RUNAWAYS

RUNAWAYS

America's Lost Youth

by
Maryanne Raphael and Jenifer Wolf

Drake Publishers Inc.   New York

Published in 1974 by
Drake Publishers Inc.
381 Park Avenue South
New York, New York 10016

Library of Congress Cataloging in Publication Data

Raphael, Maryanne.
  Runaways: America's lost youth.

  1. Runaway youth--United States. 2. Youth--Suicidal behavior. 3. Runaway
youth--United States--Case studies. I. Title.
HQ796.R364   301.43'15'0973   74-6088
ISBN 0-87749-669-2

Printed in the United States of America.

CONTENTS

Preface to Runaways

This is an important book. Nowhere else have I seen the theme of the Runaways treated as thoroughly, honestly, unflinchingly. It is important because it not only describes the various stories fully, but because it offers suggestions for improving a tragic situation. To run away is no longer the romantic escape to join a circus, a sailing ship, to see other lands. It is the young, the vulnerable, exposed to all the dangers of a criminally inclined culture. It is painful to read.

"Young people are reacting to a society that has devalued human relations, that has subordinated them to acquisitiveness and competition and that has resulted in affluence and loneliness."

Maryanne Raphael and Jenifer Wolf have been entrusted with the true story of the first impulse, the feelings, complete confessions. They have gone deeply into conditions and motivations. The individual portraits emerge vivid, in depth and complete. There is an awareness of the total problem, not just a segment of it. I feel that they understand the aspirations, the fantasies, the hungers and weakness of the young. The book is done with compassion but with a full knowledge of the extent, the enormity of the problem. The study is remarkable, because while encompassing all the tragedies and horrors which threaten the runaways, it also registers what they hungered for, what they sought, dreamed, imagined. So you become aware of how much they gambled, how much they sacrificed. And the motivation is not always negative. They are seeking another world. They do not know how to find it. In its conclusion, the book seeks to state very clearly the needs, desires, wishes and expectations of the young which set them wandering.

A million teenagers ran away from home.

The authors quote Mark Gerzon: "We who make them runaway should ask ourselves, from what kind of society are they trying to escape?"

Every aspect of the subject is thoroughly explored: the mistakes made by the lawmakers, by the parents, by the teenagers themselves.

"Laws which make the runaway a fugitive, which preclude a runaway from procuring birth control, housing and employment should be repealed."

The authors ask us: "Do not be afraid to read this book."

There is nothing to fear from confronting all the aspects of truth as well as possible solutions. The intention of the book is fulfilled: it is written so we will have full knowledge of the conflicts and fates of runaways, and a full knowledge of its meaning, its potential for the creation of a different world.

Anais Nin

RUNAWAYS

Introduction

"Dear Dad:

The establishment beat me. I'm leaving for good. I'm not going to pull a Paula trick so give me a day & call the police. I'm sorry I don't have the guts to tell you personally, but I feel I am compressed here at Buck-Walter Road and going to Great Valley.

The final thing that decided me was that last Friday I got caught smoking for the third time. After thinking all weekend, I decided it was best for everybody concerned & mostly for myself. I want to live my way & Now. This is probably the hardest thing for older people to understand because they've already lived awhile & have a completely different concept of time.

One of these days I'm going to have to pick up my stakes & anyway, from all you've shown me and taught me & under the circumstances, it's best to do it now. I know I'm leaving one of the best positions I could possibly hope to attain for my age but the other things about it make it next to impossible for my head to cope with & be me & be happy.

I hope that you feel that it is good & not bad that I am going. I won't be going up to Maine or down to Mexico as that would defeat my purpose entirely. Please don't blame anybody — including yourslef — just me.

I still love you and Orin and Jo Anne & everybody else & I will write.

Love,

your son
Teig"

Why do children run away? The obvious answer is that they're unhappy at home. Very often, their reasons for leaving would seem more than adequate by anyone's standards.

The majority of them, however, don't leave behind notes that explain why they are going away. They just disappear.

Many runaways come from homes where a parent or another adult beats them brutally or exploits them sexually, where daily they are in physical danger. It has been estimated that four out of every five children admitted to emergency rooms are victims of such abuse or neglect and deprivation because an adult alcoholic or drug addict drinks up or shoots up all of the family resources and the child cannot count on getting even enough to eat.

Sometimes the circumstances are less dramatic, but still too difficult or depressing for the child who is struggling to be free, to chart an identity.

The adults in the household may be unable to provide anything but the barest necessities of food and shelter, and the child may have to hustle to satisfy his needs and desires for clothing, records, movie tickets, spending money, etc. The same unrelenting poverty may drive the adults so harshly that they are too beleaguered, too weary and dispirited to give the child the attention, affection, and understanding that he requires. On the other hand, there is often an absence of affection in a sea of material goods. So the child hits the streets in search of the things he craves, whether they be material goods or emotional fulfillment.

Frequently, two young lovers, faced by parental hostility to their relationship, run off to remain together. Parents too often feel they alone have the last say. And, maybe the main thing these and all the other runaways are saying is "No, Mom, No, Dad. We have that last say. We control our bodies."

They start off small, at a disadvantage perhaps. They look up to us, take their first faltering steps between our legs as they see how we walk, mimic our mannerisms, and observe our inconsistencies, the "un-happiness" example we set in the home with our fights and double-dealings, even as we hold onto the threading rein of child domination and the power to say no.

Communication between parent and child can be reduced to sad newspaper graffiti:

Dear Son, Martin told Fred that David spoke to you on the street last month. It was shortly before your recent 19th birthday. In fact on the day of your birthday we received two calls but never spoke to the caller. We hoped desperately it was you. The entire family loves and misses you. Please contact us in some way. Love, Mom and Dad.

Jerry S. Please call Mom and Dad. We now realize your hair wasn't important. Rufus misses you.

To Theodore H.: Dear Son, you were right. It is better this way. Both your mother and I are adjusting to your absence. Please write or call so we'll know you're okay. If you need money, we'll send what we can. Love, Mom and Dad.

Running away, for the children from the slums, the ghettos, the rundown sections of our cities, is often a gradual process. The child spends progressively less time at home and more time out on the streets or in other places where he can be among his peers. He hangs out. He window-shops for a new life, a new hardness; he learns how to cope beyond the television life. After a time, he ceases to return home altogether or comes home only sporadically.

And what about the parents' reactions at these various stages of the child's detachment from the home? In most cases, anger and strict punishments give way to reluctant acceptance when the parent realizes that he or she cannot really offer the child alternatives. Of course, the parent worries about the child, and his fears that the child will get strung out on heroin or get into trouble with the law are often justified. And when a child is from the slums, especially if he is black or Hispanic, the pranks and adventures he becomes involved in, often shrugged off as mere mischievousness in white middle-class children, are frequently considered serious crimes. One such runaway of our acquaintance was arrested and sent to reform school for sitting in a parked car and pretending to drive it, even though it must have been obvious to the arresting officer that the boy had no intention of stealing it. He had been playing with the steering wheel for over an hour.

A surprising number of children run away from homes that are not poverty-stricken. They run away from wealthy homes, where not only is a great deal of money lavished on them but considerable time and attention—at least in terms of preparing them for futures envisioned by the parents. Those children run away for adventure, to enlarge the scope of their experiences, but most often because they don't see themselves in the roles their parents have laid out for them. "My parents say they want to see their daughter," we were told by one such runaway, "but I have a funny feeling they don't really see me. And they're not really interested in seeing me." Those parents who have given their children "everything" are especially hurt and confused. Newspaper ads like the following are not uncommon:

Marsha, this is your last chance. If you don't come home or at least call we will send the police after you. You broke your mother's heart. Didi keeps asking for you. How can you do this to us? You know we love you and want you with us. If you don't come back on your own I swear you will be sorry. Please don't get mad at this. We are all sick with worry. Love, Dad.

A case in point is Bonnie Bickwit, fifteen, and her boyfriend, Mitchell Weiser, sixteen. They left good homes in Brooklyn, July 27, 1973, for a weekend of rock music at Watkins Glen, New York, with six hundred thousand other "flower children" of the seventies. They, like thousands of others, never returned.

And their parents have still not given up the search; they refuse to believe that their "innocents" would run away from "everything" to nothing:

> Bonnie and Mitchell, please call home. Your parents are frantic with worry.

"We just want to know they're still alive," says Mitchell's mother. But neither parents, police, nor private investigators can find Bonnie and Mitchell, and in the underground their legend grows.

Of course, the parents' dread fear that the children may have been killed is genuine and reasonable. Witness sexual-abuse murders of Texas and the unearthing in 1973 of twenty-seven bodies from their multiple graves.

So everyone gets caught up in the act of worrying. An industry is created. When friends of Bonnie and Mitchell at John Dewey High School in Brooklyn raised $675 to help the search, it enabled the parents to hire Tracers Company of America.

But as Edward Goldfader, president of Tracers says, "There are no clues. All we can assume is that Bonnie and Mitchell are out there."

The parents have run down every alley they can think of:

1. The Police Department's Bureau of Missing Persons has checked all available sources of information.

2. The parents have mailed out thousands of MISSING circulars, very much like WANTED posters.

3. They have combed both the East and West Villages of New York City, known as cruising grounds for runaways and visited crash pads and runaway "help" centers such as Contact and Project Yes.

4. They have circulated on television news programs, appealed to the public their concern and sorrow.

5. They have mailed five hundred letters and circulars to reservations and mission schools throughout the country. Bonnie and Mitchell, like most average runaways, were interested in Indian affairs. Perhaps you remember the slave, who before slavery was abolished, ran off to join the Indians.

6. They have followed every new lead, every rumored sighting, lived in hope, sought findication. They have even visited a psychic. The two mothers went to Glen Head, Long Island, carrying with them unwashed articles of the children's clothing. The psychic felt Mitchell's polo shirt and said he sensed illness around the ear and throat. The mothers were impressed. Mitchell did have a sore throat the last time he wore the shirt.

He then felt all the clothing. The kids were in a cold area, he said, perhaps Vermont or New Hampshire. He saw Bonnie limping. The psychic needed to sleep on their letters that night. He would get in touch with the parents later. They have given up waiting to hear from him.

And how "horrible" are these kids?

According to a teacher who was faculty adviser to the Have-a-Heart Committee that raised $675, Bonnie and Mitchell were "two extremely articulate, extremely intelligent, socially involved youngsters."

"They cared about all the causes." Bonnie's mother told a reporter. "They rang bells for McGovern, they were active in an ecology program, and Bonnie helped out at a kindergarten in an elementary school.

She was very sensitive. One summer she went to Chicago and saw how animals were slaughtered. She vowed she would never eat meat again."

In retrospect, she acknowledges there was faulty communication between herself and Bonnie who went braless and loved to wear polo shirts and jeans, who refused shelves in her room and loved to keep all her possessions and all her clothes in cartons, who loved to play the radio all night, who wrote a theme paper entitled "Is the Traditional Marriage Dying?" concluding that "people are looking for alternatives to traditional ways, other ways of being happy." Bonnie, who wanted most of all to be always "sweet sixteen" with Mitchell and ran away from camp to join him—the same Mitchell whose mother tried to talk him out of being a vegetarian and would nag him to brush his teeth, whose parents didn't like his long hair and who told him how they wished he wouldn't go to that rock festival, where he and Bonnie evidently decided to stay away until they could be eighteen and no longer vulnerable.

What we have here is a continuing ballad: tens of thousands of parents hoping to catch another glimpse of their lost children, awaiting a final confrontation, a reasoning; and those children running, searching, hoping to be free, discovering America, savoring the ingredients that make ours a bountiful yet cold and violent nation where you can grow up or down. You just have to keep moving fast because here things do move fast, carrying with them events and people and exposing our kids to the ecstasy, heartbreak, and changeling furies of a country in perpetual motion.

As you can see, if you're a parent reading this, and you have a Bonnie or a Mitchell on your mind, you have a world of company. Consider the current figures. Conservatively estimated, there are at least seven hundred thousand runaways. During 1973, in New York City alone, the police were notified of 14,171 runaways under the age of 18—more than eight thousand of them are girls.

And what about the unreported ones or those who turn eighteen and run off, never to return? Thousands have vanished into the closed circles of religious groups or Satanic cults, communes experimenting in new life-styles, some Utopian; or political bands at war with the system and all the things their parents hold dear.

What about a twenty-year-old Patty Hearst who brands her father, newspaper magnate Randolph A. Hearst, "corporate liar" and enters into league with her kidnappers, who assumes a new name, Tania (that of Che Guevara's companion in the hills of Bolivia), after sixty days in captivity and turns her back on the man she was about to marry, telling him: "We both know what really came down that Monday night but you don't know what's happened since then. I have changed, grown. I've become conscious and can never go back to the life we led before. What I am saying may seem cold to you and to my old friends, but love doesn't mean the same thing to me any more.

"My love has expanded as a result of my experiences to embrace all people. It's grown into an unselfish love for my comrades here, in prison and on the streets. A love that comes from the knowledge that no one is free until we are all free!"

And, after announcing that she has chosen to stay with the Symbionese Liberation Army, Miss Hearst concluded: "One thing which I learned is that the corporate ruling class will do anything in their power in order to maintain their position of control over the masses, even if this means the sacrifice of one of their own.

"It should be obvious that people who don't even care about their own children couldn't possibly care about anyone else's children. The things which are precious to these people are their money and power, and they will never willingly surrender either, and people should not humiliate themselves by standing in lines in order to be fed, nor should they have to live in fear of their lives and the lives of their children."

What about the sensational stories that never come to our notice?

The myth of the American melting pot has become a reality. Everywhere kids from the slums and suburbs share their "pot", their brown rice, their experiences. United by their youth, their status as fugitives, their consciousness of themselves as a "Third World," and their poverty, they reject parent-imposed age limitations on the explorations of humanity.

Anyone under eighteen unable to prove that he or she is living with a parent or guardian is living outside of the law, a fugitive. Police can detain and question teen-agers simply because they are on the streets late at night. If they happen to be runaways, usually they are forcibly returned to their parents. But if Mom and Dad don't want them, and no acceptable adult comes forward to accept the responsibility for their livelihoods, they may be sent to a reform school.

Lydia, Come home, dear. Mother found the ring & asks you
to forgive her for suspecting you. Your dog misses you. We all
do. We need your bright smile to make our house a home.
Come back to us. Love, Mother and Daddy.

Some parents allow their children to be sent up the hill by default. Like
Pontius Pilate, they wash responsibility off their hands and sulk in
memory lanes. Others try hard to mend the broken fences of their homes.

The decks are stacked for the exceptions. We once knew a petite,
vulnerable-looking little girl who was sent to reform school seven times,
simply because her parents failed to show up in court after she was picked
up for loitering. Finally, despite the hassle and stress of her growing-up,
like a lotus bursting through the mud to bloom, she managed to attach
herself to a young couple with two small children. They offered her room,
board, and protection from police harassment in exchange for
baby-sitting. She gladly accepted this very temporary solution to her
problem.

Police not only pick up children on the street without any evidence of
their having committed a crime, but they also break into apartments and
crash pads that appear to have transient populations of young people, in
their search for runaways and drugs. Some parents claim that their
children are incorrigible and impossible to control and actually request
that they be sent to juvenile jails. One runaway says that his mother was
"naive enough to believe she was sending me to reform school for my
own good."

There are parents, of course, (or parent-substitutes) who are more
severe. One runaway's aunt, her legal guardian, felt that her charge
deserved to go to either a detention home or reform school because of her
"shameless behavior" - she let young men know she was attracted to
them. Some parents have sent their "difficult, strong-headed, rebellious"
children to mental institutions to cure them of such disorders as failure to
advance rapidly in school, the cultivation of "disreputable" friends,
disapproval of the parents' values, and the sin of all sins, a complete
rejection of their life-styles and bringing-down-the-barn on all their
dreams.

However, kids escape from institutions just as they do from parents
and foster homes. What are the options when they bring off these great
escapes? Runaways who grew up in the slums tend to remain in the slums,
circulating perhaps throughout neighborhoods or moving to similar ghettos
in other parts of the same city. Middle-class runaways tend to be more
mobile, partly because they are more often fleeing from parents who can
afford the luxury of pursuit. But they, too, usually settle in slum areas,
especially in larger cities that provide a degree of anonymity.

Some homeless kids, especially those who were thrown out (not an unusual phenomenon), find shelter in doorways and on rooftops, or they may sleep on nearby beaches or in subways. But sooner or later, in most parts of the country, they must seek indoor shelter. Generally, people under eighteen can't rent apartments even if they have the money, and most runaways don't have the money. Crash pads are a common solution to the problem of shelter. The legal tenant, over eighteen usually, may or may not remain in residence while transient runaways and other young people, street people, or college dropouts, move in and out of the place over a period of months or years. The rent is shared by those who happen to be living there when the time comes to pay it. They often find each other through ads such as the following:

Family of freaks looking for house with elbow room.

For the homeless-I am 22-year-old male Communist writer. I would feel much safer if I had a roommate. No rent will be charged if you can cook and are willing to do light housework. Though I'd prefer a Communist like myself, if you can cope with my political beliefs, I'll return the favor.

People wanted! Not rats for the rat race. Intentional Communities now forming. For city and rural co-ops. Seattle, Washington.

How do those youngsters support themselves? How do they obtain food and other necessities? To a large extent, they do without. Or they steal, especially food and clothing, but books and records are also much in demand. They often take pride in successful "rip-offs." They look upon stealing from stores, especially, grocery chains and department stores, as different from stealing from individuals; they see it simply as thinning out the surplus, feeding the people. Everything belongs to everybody. Down with monopolies and money games.

They might beg, usually in the neighborhoods in which they have settled, although some runaways are more enterprising and station themselves in the wealthier sections of town, commercial areas, or places frequented by tourists, whever there are people with more money who have not been hardened to panhandlers.

We were introduced to one runaway who had become a real pro at panhandling and had gained wide fame among her peers for having raised it to such an art on so regular a basis. She was not put off by rejection; she just smiled and endured. She accepted the reality that there was bound to be more misses than hits, and many were the times she made enough to feed the eleven persons who shared her commune. And she was only fourteen years old.

Others are less resourceful:

> Fallen Angel. Will commit atrocities. Call after midnight. Ask for Sebastian.

> Well built, young black stud needs bread fast. Will do anything, repeat, anything for a quick buck. No inhibitions.

> Please "HELP". Urgent. Any donation very welcome. Send to "Help" c//o this paper.

The runaways find it difficult, if not impossible, to get jobs because it is illegal to hire people under eighteen without working papers, and working papers usually require parental consent. And, even if the child can get working papers, most employers shun the likely hazard of police involvement. Some are fortunate enough to obtain off-the-record jobs such as baby-sitting or assisting with craft work. Still others try peddling, although this is risky since police frequently harrass peddlers of any age, with or without a license.

Dealing in drugs is another opportunity to make money and a way of obtaining free drugs as well. Many, if not most, runaways have been into drugs since long before they left home. In fact, it may have been one of the causes of friction between the child and his parents.

Ours is, after all, an alcoholic- and drug-oriented society, and our children are right there behind us. Although we may cast the ferocious eye, they want their kicks, too. Is Indian incense floating out of Danny's room, is he nodding at the dinner table, eating in his room, skipping classes? Are you relieved that he's into wine and not the dreaded marijuana leaf? But do you have the guts to tell him not to drink too much, what is right and what is wrong, to define that narrow path to wholesomeness and real belonging? Kids run away from lack of guts, and search for other heroes that will provide them with the meaning and direction they need in order to be inspired on to productive lives.

They can make a bad choice. Teen-agers from inner-city slums, for example, often gravitate toward dealing because the drug dealers that they see on the block have more money than the other neighbors and know how to flaunt it. And kids begin using drugs because their friends do.

Drug dealers are eager to sell youngsters heroin, barbituates, and amphetamines. Once the youngsters are hooked, they will be steady customers, willing to do just about anything to get a fix, including mugging, housebreaking, prostitution, and ripping-off friends and relatives for their money or any possessions that can be pawned. Often they themselves become dealers in their turn and lure other kids into addiction.

Pimps, like dealers, attempt to get teen-age girls addicted to narcotics so that they will have to hustle to support their habits. Pimps also frequently abduct young girls and beat them or threaten other acts of violence in order to force them into prostitution and live off their earnings.

And, right behind the pimps and dealers who abuse runaways and exploit them for profits are the assorted rapists, sadists, flimflam freaks, sordid bounty-hunters, and murderers who hang around port authority buildings and other places where runaways can be spotted and lured off with the promise of a place to stay, or simply a kind word and that special neon flash of a city smile and a polished strut. In *Runaways* you will meet two girls who were kidnapped by pimps and held prisoner in a house in Q ueens! And a young boy who was raped by a "gentleman" who offered him a place to stay.

Sometimes other runaways will perpetuate the exploitation. There is on record one young man who had a series of young girls staying at his place. He would pick them up outside music halls, juice bars, and ice-cream parlors. The girls, often only thirteen or fourteen, would feel obligated to exchange sex for a place to stay and possibly a meal.

Yes, it's a hard life.

But we also have the good Samaritans, the concerned. Runaways are often aided in their day-to-day struggle both by other runaways and by older individuals in the communities where they live. There are also organizations that attempt to deal with the problems without the mercenary goals of Tracers, in some of the larger cities. These centers are underfunded, understaffed, and hamstrung by laws that govern the young fugitive.

"There used to be two places for runaways to run to,"says Tony Romeo, former head of the Village Project, a mental-health clinic on the lower East Side, "haight'Ashbury and the East Village. Now there's hardly a city in the country that doesn't have its special area of freaks.

"What this development means to young runaways is that it's harder to find help. With them scattered all over the country, they are less noticeable as a problem. That's one of the reasons they are now being forgotten or dismissed as not being such an urgent problem as, say, Watergate."

According to Peter Haynes, a former supervisor of Boston's Sanctuary Hostel, "kids complain of being drugged and forced to submit to all sorts of atrocious acts. The media doesn't bring this out. The public only thinks of street people through such events as Woodstock, when it looks like they're on vacation."

"The kids don't trust the established agencies," we were told by Brian Slattery, head of San Francisco's Huckleberry House, which was started in 1967 and is probably the oldest runaway center still in existence. "our ultimate hope is to show them a way to meet their needs in ways that are acceptable."

In Chicago, Gerda Flanigan operates "Looking Glass Center." Its manual reads: "In extreme cases get the client to the nearest hospital, but try to get dope off the client before he gets to the hospital. This will avoid a bust."

In Texas, Operation Peace of Mind enables runaways to contact their parents indirectly by phone to assure them that they are all right or at least still among the living.

> My mother and father fucked me up, but now that I've split I'm getting my head back together. Don't fall for the shit your parents hand you, fight back. Putting down momism is the first step to breaking the Establishment.

Of course, there is the romantic tradition of running away from home to join the Navy or the circus, to become a movie star, to elope. There is also the literary tradition of running away exemplified by Huck Finn, Peter Pan, and the lost boys. In the middle and late sixties, it became apparent that runaway teen-agers had become a social rather than an isolated phenomenon, a promise both true and false. The growing number of middle- and upper-class runaways captured the imagination of the media, and soon children of affluent or at least comfortable contemporary, nuclear families were leaving home in droves, lured by the media's representation of the freedom, beauty, and excitement of the hippie culture:

The media, for all its slants and distortions, was reflecting the very real exuberance and optimism of the period. The new political awareness that had begun with the Civil-Rights movement of the late fifties and early sixties was taking even firmer hold with a massive opposition to American military involvement in South-east Asia. A great cry arose against American oppression and exploitation, particularly of nonwhite populations both inside and outside its borders.

At the same time, the spread of psychedelic drugs throughout the youth culture, which began also in the fifties with the beats, promised expanded consciousness through . eightened sensory perception and a more profound emotional life. And, of course, the models for the new expanded consciousness were the very people who had been barred from the "American way of life," which no longer appealed to large numbers of American youth, partly because it appeared to be based on greed and hypocracy and partly because it threatened to preclude emotional growth through experience.

It all seemed to fit together, and it still does; only the momentum of our optimism seems to have been lost, and more of our youngsters with it:

I.D. wanted. Female, 5'2" 120 pounds. Out of state preferred.

Send $1 to Clyde.

Larry O., call home. Uncle Morris died and left you the gold watch you always loved. We all miss you and are worried out of our minds. Please, please call or better yet come home. Alice was asking for you. Love.

Mary Reinholz, in a recent article in the magazine section of the New York *Daily News* calls today's runaways the "Throwaway Children." She says that most of them come from poor families where they were abused, neglected, unwanted. She describes the horrifying details of their stark struggles for survival, drug addiction and prostitution, mugging and being mugged, stealing and being ripped-off themselves. They are tougher than the middle-class runaways of the middle and late sixties, and although they may accept poverty, they certainly don't choose it. In fact the implication is that what these kids want — steady jobs, monogamous relationships, and the like — is precisely what the runaways of the sixties rejected.

In a way, the throwaways have always been with us. Historically and throughout the world, vicissitudes of urban poverty have always yielded a high proportion of unwanted children. Who among us has not wept for Oliver Twist and his cohorts?

During the middle sixties, throwaways tended to merge with flower children, in reality as well as in the media. During the middle and late sixties, in the East Village were many kids wandering around whose backgrounds resembled those of the throwaways. Paradoxically, they tended to be more sympathetic to their neglectful, even abusive, parents than were their middle-class peers. They often considered their parents "brainwashed," rarely evil. Middle-class runaways, on the other hand, were more apt to seize on any evidence of repressiveness or insensitivity on their parents' part as justification for having left home, and thus rationalized away the temptation to return to a much cushier environment than the one they now lived in. There are still middle-class runaways trying to make it "with a little help from their friends" in run-down sections of cities all over the country, but they are a much smaller proportion of the total number and tend to merge with the throwaways.

Most of the kids trying to make it on the streets today are out there because they have little or no choice. There are several reasons for this, the most important among them the deepening depression of the past few years. It's more crowded than it used to be at the fringes of the economy and the runaway, with his lack of experience and fugitive status, is likely to get squeezed fastest.

If Third-World people and women are second-class citizens; if they don't have the protection and patronage of adults, they get kicked around.

> Free, Free just to be free. High, High I want to get high. . .Write Sharon.
>
> Anyone interested in building a huge tower to Heaven to pull God down and ask him why he's making such a mess of things, please call Ronnie.

What do runaways, and youth in general, want most? It is pointless to label their desires hippie or straight, or to classify them as action-seeking or security-oriented. The thing they desire most—what most people want for themselves, and what the youngsters' vulnerable situation makes them particularly conscious of lacking—is a greater degree of control over their own lives. They want answers to questions not yet intellectualized. Many are seeking gurus, joining religious communes, Hari Krishna groups, becoming "Jesus Freaks," studying astrology and Satanism.

They want love, understanding, friendship, independence, fun, adventure, money, a certain amount of security. They want to change the world, to enjoy sex or drugs without guilt, to find fulfillment, a way to live their lives meaningfully and constructively, their own life-style.

What can we do to help young people, runaways in particular, to achieve this greater degree of control over their lives? As individuals, we can stop treating them like lepers. Among the assorted predatory individuals roaming the streets of our cities, there are, of course, some runaways. But we shouldn't assume that all young people not under the supervision of "competent" adults have only nefarious purposes. The attitude of New Yorkers toward the patrons of the juice bars that proliferated in New York a few years ago, luring the teen-age trade who could not go to regular clubs and discotheques serving liquor, is one embarrassing example of this.

When we come across runaway neighbors or friends of our children, we can offer whatever help our time and resources permit. If we have the training and inclination, we can do so as professionals or as volunteers in runaway centers and free clinics that serve street people. We cannot afford to remain indifferent to bills that would provide money to feed, house, counsel, and educate runaways. The Runaway Youth Act, which would provide ten million dollars for three years for such purposes, has twice passed through the Senate and then been rejected in the House of Representatives. It's time we let our "representatives" know how we feel, that there is a desperate need for this bill and others like it that will ensure runaways housing that resembles youth hostels rather than reform schools. Pressure should also be put on local governments to provide funds for extensive services to runaways.

Laws that make the runaway a fugitive, that do not permit them access to birth control, housing, and employment, should be repealed. Perhaps the whole concept of a "legal age" should be revised. Kids must come to be thought of as people, or the next big movement in the U.S.A. will go down in history as Children's Liberation.

The following chapters recount the stories of ten runaways and their friends. Their backgrounds are varied. They are children of the very poor, and the very rich, and of those who have achieved a borderline economic security. They come from a variety of ethnic groups. Some fled from illiterate parents and others, intellectual. Their experiences as runaways vary, too, but not nearly as much as their backgrounds.

Some of the runaways whose stories are told here left home back in the fifties. Others are of mid- and late-sixties vintage. They are now adults. Some of our runaways are out on the streets right now, hustling in order to survive another day. They resemble their predecessors and yet differ from them for today has never been done before.

We have created the much-touted global village; distances between points have become shorter or no longer exist. Our environment expands even as it breaks up. Similarly, both maturity and desperation are speeded up in our young. Leaving home isn't seen as running away; it's merely going somewhere else. The corner candy store is everywhere. Hamburgers and hot dogs taste the same all over.

Action defines meaning. They teach us, through their simplicity, bravery, and optimism, and have much to learn from us in patience, restraint, and the vast sweep of history that rights everything in its own time. Although their greatest "beef" is that we too willingly accept this history and its mishaps and ask no unusual questions because we fear tumultuous answers, they do not and therein lie both their weakness and their strength.

1
Shadow

One hot summer night in 1965, my old man answered the door to find standing there a tall, dark man dressed all in black. Behind him, like bodyguards, stood four Puerto Rican teen-agers wearing T-shirts and faded blue jeans.

"Want to buy a record player? he asked conspiratorially.

Our stereo had just been stolen so we invited them in so that we could get a look at the merchandise and see if it was ours.

It wasn't. But we had an apartment full of records we'd never listened to and decided to play them that night.

They introduced themselves as the Young Savages. We offered them some beer. They relaxed on our threadbare carpet, and after a brief comparison of our tastes in music, began recounting some of the jobs they had pulled.

When we told them we'd been robbed, they promised to find the thief and return our possessions. "And you doesn't have to worry about getting ripped off ever again," they assured us. "We're gonna spread the word you's our friends and nobody will dare touch your shit."

They asked us if we knew anyone we didn't like who owned a record player, radio, typewriter, or any of the other objects that had been stolen from us. "We'll break into their pad and get you anything you needs."

We thanked them for their offer, but said we didn't know anyone we disliked enough to do that to.

This was how I met Shadow, the first of many runaways I was to come to know during my years as a denizen of the lower East Side.

Shadow was fifteen years old then. He did not have much in common with the middle-class hippie runaway of the sixties popularized by the media for their flamboyant life-style, flower-power attraction, and the carnival atmosphere that they so often created with their spectacular clothing, psychedelics, be-ins, and demonstrations. Rather he resembles the throwaways more likely to be ignored by the media, just as they are often neglected by their parents. They don't attempt to disguise the somber appearance of poverty, or if they do, it's to try to get a straight job on which their survival may depend. There is not even the barest possibility of falling back on the soft cushion of parental affluence.

Shadow kept dropping by our apartment, and soon we became close friends. He told us he'd been born in Harlem, had two brothers and three sisters. His father was an alcoholic who frequently beat up his mother. "But I digs him more than her," he quickly added. "He's always laying bread on me and she's always asking for some of it to buy food and shit for the house."

"My friends all calls me Shadow," he said, "because I always wears black."

Shadow was the only black member of the Young Savages, a Puerto Rican gang. "I joined for protection," he told us. "I doesn't really trust them guys. They's always talking Puerto Rican and I never knows when they's talking about me. But they likes me. They knows I's a good fighter and I needs somebody to back me up.

"Them cats I hangs around with ain't really friends, not in the real sense of the word. Man, they is all Puerto Rican and when two of them gets together, they starts rattling off that gibberish and I ain't got the first guess what they's saying. Now, how is a cat going to feel close to foreigners like that?

But life is pretty rough these days," he said. "You's got to have backers if you wants to make it.

"I's the only American in the Savages. Only reason I's in is if you ain't a gang member, man, you can't even walk the streets.

"Let me tell you something what happened to me back in Harlem before I joins my first gang. I's twelve years old, see, and just starts getting hot pants for chicks.

"There's this one doll I really digs, sharp little spade chick almost dark as me. Well, one night we's coming home from a flick. It's a groovy night, summer, and there's a big mothering moon in the sky, big as a Halloween pumpkin. I's got my chick's paw, and we's grooving behind each other.

"Man, about ten big cats appears. They just drops out of the dark like hot turds and starts to surround us.

"I tells my chick to cut out. But she really digs me. So she say 'I's sticking with you, baby.' Man, you know, spade chicks is not made like ofay chicks. Spade chicks knows how to take care of theirselves. They learns quick or they ain't around to need no care.

"So my doll and me is going at these ten studs with arms and legs, hitting, kicking, scratching. She's a boss fighter. But we can't take care of all ten.

"They's laying into our cakes. Man, they beats the goodies out of me. And I got fifteen dollars on me at the time. They takes the bread off me.

They they lays into my chick. Right there in front of me, man. Everyone of them mothering bastards mounts her. They tears the hell out of her. Then they all splits.

"Somebody find us on the street and they calls a cop. The cop take us to the hospital. Man, when I gets out of the hospital, I talks to my friend Lucky what is a member of a gang. I says, 'Lucky, your gang got a opening?'

"He say, 'I doesn't know, Jackson. I's gonna check with the captain.'

"He comes back and tells me I's got to come with him to the meeting Saturday night and let the gang look me over and see if there's a opening.

"I tells my old lady I's joining a gang. I's tired of getting my balls beat. I needs protection.

"The old lady break up bawling. She say, 'It ain't good belonging to no gang. I doesn't want no boy of mine being no member of no gang. First thing I knows the cop put you in jail or worst. One night they knocks on my door and brings you in stone cold. No sir, my son ain't going to belong to no gang.'

"I stomps out of the crib. My old lady done saw what them studs does to a cat what ain't got no backing. If she think I's going to make that scene again she done flipped her turnip.

"I meets my friend Lucky and he take me to this old garage where the gang hold their meetings. Lucky introduce me to the captain.

"The captain say, 'What your name, man?'

"I says 'Jackson.'

"He say, 'I doesn't like it. Give me your first name.'

"I says 'Wilmar' 'cause that's my name.

"He shake his head. 'You's all in black so I's going to call you Shadow.'

"I says, 'But I doesn't like Shadow.'

" 'That don't matter,' he say. 'I likes it. From now on you's Shadow.'

And that name's stuck with me ever since. I still doesn't like it. Makes the chicks think I's a jitterbug. But I's used to it now.

"Well, the captain say, 'Come here, Shadow,' and he take me into the next room. All the gang members is lined up in there.

" 'We has to see you in action,' the captain say, 'so you pick out which member of the gang you wants to take on.'

"Man, I looks around the room and doesn't like what I sees. There's about twenty studs lined up there, studs of all sizes, and right in the center I sees a mug I recollect, then another and another.

"Man, it's them ten cats what's laid into me and my chick's cakes. I asks them doesn't I know them from somewhere. They all ten shakes their turnips no.

"I says to myself, 'You doesn't know me, maybe, but I knows you and when I gets me some back-ups I's going to see that you knows me.'

"Anyway, that ain't really the problem at the minute. The problem is which stud I's going to pick to fight. I figures if I picks a small cat he just may lick me and I's going to look stupid and nobody gonna give me no credit if I licks him. So I points a digit at the biggest mothering stud in the line.

"Man, I's so scared the piss is ready to spurt out but I lays into the big stud. He come back hard with a dig at my left eyeball and another right away.

"I lays into him again. But I's already feeling dizzy. So I gets directly under the mother and he jab at my top. His fist digging in my skull.

"I feels better. He fall for it. My skull's harder than his fist. He's laying into my cap and I knows his paw is hurting worse than my cap. I just stands still and takes it.

"Then when I figures his paw is too screwed up to do any more damage, I lays into his cakes, really lets him have it. Right side of the jaw. Left side. Man, I's got him spinning. Finally he take a lucky swing and send me flying across the floor.

"The captain say, 'That's it, boys,' and everybody start clapping.

" 'You knows how to stand your own, Shadow. If you digs the gang, you's in.'

" 'I digs, man.' "

"Let me tell you, I ain't had me no more trouble once I joins me a gang. That is, no trouble being jumped on the street. I's got me some back-up now and the gangs knows me. Ain't nobody going to mess with Shadow now or they got a gang on their tail.

"The cats in the gang digs me right from in front. So, soon as I gets enough men I knows I can count on, I tells them how them ten studs done jumped me and my chick. Then says them ten cats is members and blood brothers but they needs them a lesson in how to be neighborly.

"So we corners them one by one and lays into them and collects their bread and all together we gets seventy-five bucks and we buys a couple nickels and gets stoned.

"But them ten studs doesn't hold it against us. They just tells me things is square now."

The runaways in the sixties felt no need to join a gang except under special circumstances. One reason for this was their strong sense of belonging to the well-established counter-culture of youth. They saw themselves as connected with people of their age group all over the world who shared the same life-style, the same tastes in clothes, music, art, and food, the same moral values and goals. A good many runaways still feel this way.

Earlier runaways, especially those from minority groups in ghetto neighborhoods, did not have this sense of belonging. They did not leave home with the great expectation of finding a group of their peers who shared their basic ideas and would welcome them with open arms. And, things are not too different for today's throwaways who come from minorities, poor families, foster homes, orphanages, mental institutions, and the like. They see themselves as pretty much alone out there, facing the world on their own. Some of them therefore still seek out the cloak of gang membership. Witness the recent upsurges of gang bouts on the lower East Side and in other big-city ghettos where the throwaways congregate.

For example, when Shadow left Harlem for the East Village, a short subway ride downtown, he might as well have gone across country. He had no friends or acquaintances at first and felt just as alienated as he would have in Denver or San Francisco.

One night Shadow told us why he had run away from home.

"My life is going smooth until my old lady tell me my old man done knocked her up again. There we is, five kids and two parents crowded into four rooms and they goes and makes another kid. Man, was I pissed.

"My old man was getting drunk every night and laying into my old lady. That made me mad as hell. I doesn't like to see him beating the shit out of her. But he were over six-foot tall and there weren't nothing I could do to stop him.

"Then I starts looking at the good side, hoping maybe he's gonna make her lose the kid. But he keep beating her and that kid just ain't letting go.   Her stomach get bigger and I makes up my mind I's splitting before the place get so crowded I can't turn around.

"I takes me a few bucks from my old lady's purse and splits."

Even before leaving home, Shadow had felt the need to join a gang for protection and a sense of belonging. Out on his own, his need was even greater.

He told us how he became a member of the Savages.

"First time I done focus my eyeballs on the lower East Side, I says to myself, 'Shadow, this ain't no good neighborhood. This is a bad place. There's gangs on every corner. Most of them is speaking Puerto Rican. They can be planning to bump me off and I's standing right next to them and doesn't know it.'

"So I decides this time I's going to play it smart. I's going to find me a gang before they finds me.

"I sees this Puerto Rican stud standing on the corner digging the sounds from a big portable transistor radio he carrying. I walks over to him and asks can I buy him a beer.

"He say, 'Sure.' We goes in the grocery and I gets him a Miller's and a pack of Pall Malls. Then, while he's drinking, I asks him, 'Hey, man, you know is there a gang located round here?'

"He say, 'What you want to know that for?' and he don't sound friendly.

"I says, 'I is new on the block. Where I comes from I belongs to a gang and I wants to join me another one.'

"He want to know the name of my old gang. 'The Savages,' I tells him. When I says that he just about flip his wig.

"He say, 'Man! That's the name of our gang. Right now our captain looking for a cat name of Shadow. You sees them signs on the wall?'

"He point to *Shadow* what is written all over the building and say, 'We had us a cat named Shadow, but he goes and gets hisself sent away for a long term. So we's looking for a cat to take his place.'

"I says, 'Man, you kidding me. My gang name is Shadow.'

"Do he look scared then. He 'bout bust his brain. Like something funny happening.

" 'I's got to take you to the captain immediately,' he say.

"Soon as we sees the captain, my new friend tell him I belongs to the Young Savages uptown and my gang name's Shadow and the captain shake my hand and say, 'Shadow, you's in, man.'

"I ain't got to fight nobody this time. Just like that, I gets me some backers."

Although gangs have been notorious for getting kids into desperate situations, many social workers have found it easier to work with gangs than with individual troubled youngsters. Gangs do fulfill certain basics, such as the need for a family and a system of immediate visible authority. They have helped many poor and neglected children develop enough self-confidence to try to make something of themselves.

Shadow's experiences with the Young Savages were beneficial in that they filled a vacuum in his life. But they also contributed to his already heavy load of problems.

The Savages spent most of their time borrowing cars that were parked on our street without permission from their owners, of course, then driving them around and returning them to their original position if another car hadn't parked there in the meantime.

Shadow told me of some of the situations the gang got into:

"I guess I oughts to think about it before replacing a cat what's in the tombs. What's to protect me from any leftover bad luck that's hanging around?

"Sure enough, about two weeks after I steps into this cat's shoes I's standing on the corner digging this white chick and some of the gang comes up to me and say, 'Come on, Shadow. Something's up.'

"I ain't interested in no rumble at the minute. I's grooving behind this chick so I gets the address and tells the cats I be there later.

"I stays with the chick til she's got to split. Then I makes it down to the spot, but the cats done split. So I heads back home.

"This bull car pull up at the curb and a big bull holler, 'Hey, where you going? Come over here.'

"I says, 'What you want with me, man? I ain't done nothing. I's just walking.'

" 'Get in the car,' the big bull say.

"I figures there ain't no use running so I gets in the bull car. The bulls drives me to the bull crib. They takes me to a little room and the big bull say, 'Okay, kid, sit down.'

"I sits and he say, 'What's your name?'

" 'Wilmar Jackson.'

" 'Okay, Wilmar,' he say, 'You ready to talk?'

'I ain't got nothing to say. I's already told you I ain't done nothing.'

"He ask, 'What you doing hanging around Houston Street?'

" 'I done told you I was just walking, going home.'

"There's five bulls in the room. But the big stud what pulled me in is doing all the talking. He's getting mad. He say, 'Look, boy. Stop wasting our time. We got more important matters to deal with. Tell us about the grocery you guys held up.'

" 'I ain't held up no grocery. I just took my chick home and I was going to my crib.'

" 'A likely story,' the little bull who drive the car say.

"Another bull, a short stud with blond hair and lots of muscles, say, 'Listen, black boy. You going to talk or we got to make you talk?'

" 'I done told you I ain't done nothing.'

"The blond stud lay his fist in my cakes. He give me a real going-over. The rest of the bulls watches him.

"The big bull what picked me up try to play nice. 'What you doing hitting that little boy? Don't you know he's a good boy?' Then he lay into me.

"After them bulls finishes with me, I's all bloody. I got me a black eye, a cut on my cap, and bruises all over. But I ain't talking. Man, I's so hung up when I seen them bulls I doesn't think to get rid of the shit. You should see them studs when they finds the joints. They looks like kids at Christmas.

" 'So you won't talk, huh? Well, them cigarettes'll talk to the judge for you.'

"Man, I's up shit creek without a paddle. Them cats books me for having pot and disorderly conduct.

"When I goes before the judge, he ask me how I got all beat up. Before I gets a chance to open my trap, a cop tell him I's that way when he pick me up. He say I been rumbling.

"The judge believe him, of course. Them judges and cops alwasy sucking each other's sticks.

⁃ "But I done made another big mistake. I's so uptight when the bulls asks me for my address, I gives them my old lady's pad in Harlem. They goes and calls her. And she come to court and tell the judge I ain't bad. I's just sick. She say I ain't right in the head and ask the judge to send me to the bughouse and not the tombs.

"She tell how when I's young I hears my old man's voice all the time when my old man is down in Mississippi.

"In them days I hears him say, 'Come up on the roof.I goes up and there ain't nobody there. He say, 'Come out in the street.' I goes out and he ain't there.

"And my old lady tell how she upt me in the nuthouse that time. She show the judge a paper from the doctors what say I ain't right.

"So the judge say I got to talk to this headshrinker.

"The shrinker ask me does I still hears my old man's voice. He want to know what my old man say.

"He say not to fight clean. Cause when I's a little cat I fights clean. I gets another cat down, I lets him go. My old man say that ain't no good. You gives the other stud a break and he break you. He ain't going to give you no breaks. *And my old man's right.* When I fights clean, I loses. The cat I got down say he give up. I lets him go. Soon as he's on his two feets, he lay into me. When he get me down he beat the hell out of my cakes.

"The shrinker ask, 'Did your father say anything else?'

" 'His trap always moving,' tells him.

" 'Do you hear voices now?' he ask.

"I says, 'Yeh.'

"The shrinker ask is it my old man's voice.

"I says, 'No man. Your voice.'

"The shrinker call the bulls and say, 'Take this boy away.'

"They puts me in the tombs in a special place for nuts. All these here studs talks to theirselvs and fights with the wall. One cat hitting the bed.

"I asks him what he doing.

" 'I's beating my old lady.'

"I tells him that ain't no old lady. That's a bed. And he say!

'Don't tell me that ain't my old lady. I knows my old lady.' And he go right on beating the bed til his fist are all bloody.

"Man, it's screwed up. We never sees no chicks. They feeds us slop. One day the cat bring me the slop. He shout, 'Get your hot rice, men!'

"I says, 'That ain't rice, man. That shit.' I grabs the bowl and dumps it on his cap.

"They comes and puts me in a room so short you can't stand up. They keeps me there for a week.

"They finally lets me out of that cell. It take me days before I gets the kinks out of my back so's I can stand up straight.

"And they puts me in a cell with another crazy cat. The first night I's in my bed we's got bunk beds. I's on the bottom bunk. Well, I can't get me no sleep. This here cat is jumping and twisting and turning. I's afraid the whole frisking bed is going to fall on top of me.

"I's laying there getting madder and madder. I looks up and sees this big piece of beef staring me in the eyeballs. Man, that cat's balling the bed and his beef is coming through the springs. That mad stud just about to come all over me.

"I's so mother mad I jumps out of bed and grabs the cat before he know what's happening I tears him out of the mattress, almost cuts off his beef. He got some beef on him. The springs scratches it so it bleeding. He lets out a howl.

"I throws him up against the wall and lays into the stud.

"When morning come, I tells the guard to get that cat out of my cell or I's going to kill him.

"They moves him to another cell. And they puts another cracked nut in with me. This cat always trying to break out. He pulling on the bars and he shouting, "Let me out of here! Let me out! Then he start beating the walls. He lay into them until his paws bleeding.

"He's a short cat but he's solid muscle. I doesn't want him to take me on. That night the mother get my toothbrush and start brushing his teeth. Using my toothpaste, too.

"When he finish brushing his teeths, he start rubbing the rest of the toothpaste in his chest. He take all the covers off my bed. I can't get him to give them back so I's got to sleep all night in that cold cell without no covers. Man, I freezes my cakes off.

"But me and that cat starts getting along real groovy. He sit around saying crazy shit. I always answers him with something even crazier and the cat can't figure me out.

"One day that cat go up to the biggest cat in the joint. He take a burning cigarette and put it out on the big cat's arm. The big cat is ready to kill him. He look up at him and say, 'Cool, it, baby. I ain't done nothing to you I doesn't do to my own self,' and he light another cigarette and put it out on his own bare chest.

"He let out a howl and run into the shower with his clothes on. The big cat don't know what to make of it. He just walk away shaking his head."

After his first experience in jail, Shadow resolved to be extra careful in order to avoid being sent back. But his affiliation with the gang made this very difficult, for it was at this time that they had begun to play dangerous games with other people's cars.

"Man, everybody what park his car in the block, the Savages jumps inside it and goes riding. They rides all around town. Then they drives the car back to the block and parks it wherever they finds a space.

"Man, if one of the cats what owns the cars come looking for it and it ain't there, he can call the bulls and they can be waiting for the Savages when they comes back to park the car.

"I tries to lay some sense on the cats. But they ain't listening. Man, the first night I comes home, Froggy jump in a Jaguar and just sit there making like he's going somewhere.

"He sit there for about an hour while the rest of us studs is flapping our jaws. This hip-looking Jap cat come out of a building and head for the Jaguar. Froggy jump out of the car and start messing around with a motorcycle parked right in front of the Jaguar.

"The Jap cat change his directions and walk up to the motorcycle. Froggy take a couple steps back and stand digging the cat. The cat examine the motorcycle real careful, then walk off.

"Froggy jump back in the Jaguar.

"All the Savages laughing. Lefty tell me Froggy just got out of the tombs hisself.

"I says he must not stayed long enough.

"Lefty say they only keeps Froggy one night but they beats the cakes off him before they lets him go and knocks out most his teeths.

"I asks them what Froggy is busted for. He's sitting in a cop's car, but he don't know it's a cop car 'cause it ain't marked. When he leave the car, he take the cop's mirror and put it in another car.

"He sitting in the other car when the cop come up. Froggy jump out and start running.

"The rest of the Savages is running around. They tells Froggy how to go to get away from the bulls. And man, he get away.

"He go home and change his shirt, put on a red cap. He come back cool as ever and climb in another car. He sit there acting like he going somewhere.

"He's still sitting in the car when the cop come by. The cop ask, 'Is this your car?'

"Froggy say he don't know. The cop ask, 'Then why you sitting there?'
"Froggy say, 'I ain't hurting the car.'
"So the cop take him away. It's the same cop whose car he's sitting in before. The cop really hot.
"Us cats doesn't expect to see Froggy again for a long stretch. But next day here he come strutting in and that night he back in the street digging all the cars.
"While we's talking, Froggy come up and offer us all some chocolates he done found in a car."

Most runaways return home after a week. The longer they stay away, the less chances there is that they'll eventually return and the more likely it is that they'll get into trouble with the law, start using or dealing in drugs, or resort to prostitution and other illegal hustles.

The first contact with the parents may come a few days or even a few hours after they leave. In Shadow's case, the police contacted his mother after he was arrested. But it was three months before he saw her on his own initiative. He was having a hard time feeding himself properly, started remembering his mother's good cooking and rich smell of it, and decided to go home.

She was happy to see him. "Where you been?' she asked. "Don't say nothing. Have something to eat. Look how skinny you got."

He was eating, "feeding my face," and looking at her out of the corners of his eyes, expecting her to throw a fit at any moment and try to keep him there, to start crying, getting her blood pressure up, begging him to stay. He couldn't bear it. The thought of a scene made him shudder.

As it turned out, there was no such scene. But he made one mistake during his visit that was his undoing.

Before I goes to see my old lady, I been smoking hash. I's stoned out of my head. She doesn't notice anything til I sits down to watch me some TV but I doesn't bother to turn it on. I's sitting there digging the scene, laughing out loud, just enjoying myself.

"My old lady decides I's crazy. She call Bellevue and them bastards comes and takes me away.

"I tells them I ain't crazy. I's just stoned. They don't pay no attention. They keeps me there until I's really crazy and sends me to Pilgrim State.

"There I gets turned on to hard stuff. Lots of cats in the nuthouse has outside contacts and always has lots of shit. They likes me and keeps saying, 'Here Shadow, have some of this.' So I stays high and doesn't mind the place so much."

Shadow has been in and out of mental hospitals ever since. As we mentioned in our introduction, many parents, middle-class and ghetto alike-send their youngsters to mental hospitals as a kind of punishment for running away or refusal to conform to their life-styles. It's very important that all such parents be made to realize that mental institutions can become a way of life. By exposing their children to this environment, they can very easily be introducing them to hard drugs-as was the case with Shadow-or to the concept of the mental hospital as a life-style not much worse than that they've found in a home with such parents. These children need exactly the opposite of what these institutions offer.

A similar situations exists when parents insist on punishing their children by sending them to reform schools or some other such institution "to teach them a lesson," even though the judge or social worker says they can return home. Sometimes the lesson the child receives in such a place is on how to live a life of crime.

The combination of actual physical hardship with intense disillusionment creates a feeling of impotence in people like Shadow. Heroin offers an escape. Their world can be transformed into a lovely cozy place in the time it takes the drug to travel from the vein to the brain. It may be a very ephemeral solution, but a drowning person doesn't think clearly.

Shadow once told me, "There's only one time in my life when I really feels happy and wasn't on drugs. It was when I had me a friend." According to Shadow, the best friend he ever had was a young middle-class white runaway named Mack. It seems the closest thing to a melting pot in present-day America is the situation of the runaway among the street children.

Although runaways come from every conceivable ethnic, economic, and social background, once they're out on their own in the streets, or at home in the crash pads or communes and the like, they all have a number of common problems. No matter how much money their parents have, and no matter how much they manage to leave home with, sooner or later money becomes a major problem and they turn to the street tricks of the others. They learn how to panhandle (beg), shack up (pay room and board with sex), garbage shop (find clothing or redeemable objects in garbage cans), pick up odd jobs, deal in drugs, shoplift, write home accounts of distress and requests for the fare home to be used for staying away.

Even if they resolve the problem of money, there are other issues of survival with which they must cope. They are all young kids out on their own, learning independence, and drugs, bad trips, unwanted pregnancies, VD, malnutrition, and so forth are all part of it.

Shadow told me the story of his relationship with Mack and his girl friend Suzi who had run away from Ohio and settled on the lower East Side. Mack was seventeen and Suzi sixteen. They were especially lucky because Suzi had learned typing in high school and had a natural talent for it, and by wearing her hair up and selecting the right kind of clothes and make-up, she was able to appear older and to thus earn enough money to rent their own apartment in a run-down building on the lower East Side.

Shadow didn't seem to know much more than this about his friends' backgrounds. When I asked him why they had run away, he said it was the old Romeo and Juliet story. Their parents didn't like them to spend too much time together and "they wants to be beatniks. But their folks is too square."

Shadow told me of his relationship with Mack and Suzi.

"I can't tell you how glad I is when this big white stud and his chick moves into the block. I can't figure out what a ofay cat with a ofay chick is doing here. It's a bad neighborhood, a bad scene.

"But I knows from in front this is a hip cat. The day he move in, he come outside and say, 'Hello, man.'

"I says, 'You talking to me?'

"And he say, 'Sure, man. Listen, you got anything to smoke?'

"I says, 'You mean a cigarette?'

"And he say, 'I only smokes one kind of cigarette.'

"I wants to make him spell it out. So I asks, 'What kind?'

"And he say, 'The groovy kind, man. The kind that don't cause cancer.'

"I digs that. Then he asks has I got any to sell.

"I says, 'I ain't got that much. But I got enough to groove behind.'

"And he say, 'Crazy,' and ask if I wants to come to his pad and smoke. He lead me up the steps to his crib.

"I asks him why he want to move to a bad neighborhood like this. He say he dig the block.

"Inside his crib, I meets his woman Suzi. She give me a wide grin and say she glad to meet me.

"I says, 'Likewise.' Then I directs my eyeballs elsewhere. I ain't aiming to give this cat the idea I wants his chick.

"Mack ain't unpacked his stuff yet. We sits down on boxes and we blows. The cat had him a groovy ax with steel strings and he play some folk songs.

"When all the bush finish, Mack and me goes out for some beer. Outside, we meets the Savages. They calls, 'Hello Shadow,' and Mack say, 'Introduce me to your friends.'

"I tells him they ain't friends. They's just acquaintances. But he want to know them, anyhow. So I introduces him and he invite the whole mothering gang to come to his crib for some booze.

"Them cats all got their mouth dripping for Mack's chick. Most of them carrying pot. We smokes more joints.

"Mack making a big mistake when he invite all them studs to his crib. They takes it for a open invite and is knocking on his door every night.

"Mack don't dig that all them cats is coming to dig his chick. He think they coming to rap with him.

"When Mack's chick go out of town for a few days I's the onliest cat what is visiting Mack.

"Mack really dig books. He got enough books to cover two walls. They's so many big words in them I can't make heads or tails, but Mack, he grooves behind them. They says things to him. He get excited and say, 'Shadow, you got to read this.'

"I sits there making like I's digging the book. I looks over at Mack and every time he turn a page I turns one. When I gets tired of turning pages in one book, I gets me another and turns pages in it.

"I starts grooving behind the action. It relax me. Man, I's hung up on it now. Every time I walks into a crib if I sees a book I picks it up and starts turning pages. Them white chicks in the Village digs my actions. They goes for a cat what grooves behind books! And I digs Village chicks.

"Only thing that bug me is they tells me to stop processing my hair and let it grow bushy. They wants me to look like I just come out of the jungle. But I digs my process. It make me look like I got real hair. If I cuts off my process and lets my hair grow out all the cats want to know what happened to Shadow.

"Mack and me has groovy times together. We digs the animals at the zoo while we is both stoned out of our minds.

"When Mack's chick come back to town, all the Savages comes back to Mack's to rap, smoke, goof off while they gaze at his chick and get in tight with her.

"One night when we is all out, Mack's crib is busted into. They takes his ax, his typewriter, his new suit what he's going to wear gig-hunting.

"Man, I's mad. I looks for the mother what broke in. I questions all the Savages. They all tells me they ain't guilty. I's still suspicious 'cause we controls the neighborhood.

"All the Savages snooping around trying to find the crook. We checks with all the fences. Ain't none of them seen none of Mack's stuff. We figures it's a junkie what done the gig. A loner. There ain't nothing we can do about it.

"Another cat bust into Mack's crib and take his watch and his chick's jewels. We is all burning. This time, too, ain't no fences got nothing.

"Then some mother rape my ten-year-old sister and I's got to go to Harlem to take care of family business, and spends two more weeks in the tombs.

"Mothering society this is where a stud can't even revenge his own sister without getting busted!

"I gets back into commission and everything settle down normal-like.

"One night me and Mack and Suzi goes to a flick. We comes home and meets the Savages sitting in front of Mack's building getting stoned.

"Mack wants us to join them. Him and me sits down on the top of some garbage cans and starts rapping. But Suzi got to work tomorrow so she say she going up to bed.

"We pass the night this way. Every once in awhile one of us goes to Mack's crib to take a leak. Suzi is stretched out on the bed sleeping. We got to pass her to get to the bedroom, so the Savages is all doing one hell of a lot of leaking.

"We hears a siren and a fire truck pull up in front of us. The angels jumps out and gets out hoses and puts up ladders right in Mack's building.

"A big crowd gather. A bull car pull up and them cats tells everybody to go home, but we tells them we lives here.

"Mack tell me, 'Shadow, we better make sure Suzi is all right.'

"The other Savages is jealous 'cause they wants to see Suzi again in her night rags.

"When we gets to Mack's crib, the door is open. He yell, 'Suzi!'

"The crib is empty. Ain't no one on the floor seen Suzi. Mack say, 'Maybe she heard the firemen, got scared, and went up to see our friends on the next floor.'

"We goes up there and finds her. She's bawling. 'Suzi, what happened?'

"Suzi tell us she been raped. She wake up and somebody getting into bed. It's dark and she think it's Mack. The stud hit her across the face and say if she make any noise he going to kill her. She get scared. The stud is boozed up. He's having a hard time getting it up and keep slugging her, cursing like it's her fault. She don't know who the stud was. But he got a Spanish accent.

"Mack put his arms around Suzi. 'Don't worry, baby,' he say, 'we'll get him. Come on, Shadow.'

The angels is still in the building. Mack ask them what's happening. They say there's a mattress what is burning but it's under control now. They's just checking to make sure there ain't no more fire before they cuts out.

"Mack and me tells the Savages what's happened to Suzi. We all goes hunting.

" 'He's far away now,' Froggy says.

" 'That's right,' I tells Mack.

" 'Damn! I wanted to cut off that mother's balls, 'Mack say. 'I wanted to stomp the stud to death with my army boots.'

"Suzi keep begging Mack to split after that. But Mack say he got to find that stud what raped his chick before he could cut out.

"Mack's a big cat and I ain't got no doubt he can kill the cat if we finds him. But I knows them Puerto Rican cats stick together and if Mack take on one, he take on all. I tells him to lay off. 'The best thing is to split the scene.'

" 'I'll split all right,' mack said, 'after I make sure that cat pays his dues.'

"Listen, man,' I says, 'if you touches that cat you got every Puerto Rican in the neighborhood after your balls. You knows we's the minority here. And even if you can handle the P.R.'s you still got the bulls on your ass. Man, they can put you in the tombs for life if they doesn't give you the chair if you kills that stud.'

"Mack's chick say, 'He's right, Mack. I'm so tired of this shit. I don't want no more trouble.'

"So me and Suzi talks him into splitting.

"I helps them pack.

"I hates to see my friend leaving. But I knows that's the best move.

"When they was leaving, Mack pat me on the back and say, 'It's been great, Shadow. Stay cool!'

"I never seen my friend again. But I's glad he split. Can't tell what would happen if he stayed. Like I said before, it's a bad neighborhood."

After Mack left, Shadow's only friends were the other members of the Savages. They were heavy into marijuana and hash. Shadow, struggling for companionship and acceptance, tried his best to keep up with the fire and smoke. Soon he found himself back in Pilgrim State Hospital.

So for Shadow it was in and out, and in again and back to the loony bin, caring less and less about what happens to him. His days were spent in drug transit, standing at corners and watching the crowds go by, not knowing or caring; aware only of the police, who represented that other world, a hostile world that speaks a different language, an unhip scene of binding chains, men in white hospital suits, and impatient uptight doctors.

"Gimme a smoke, man." Up went the "smoke" and the genie would come out, entertain him for a moment, and instead of being merely Shadow, he'd become the essence. Nothing mattered, not even when he didn't know the name of the President of his country. What country?

But there were times when he'd know and feel and the pain became too great.

"It's them damn drugs," he'd tell me, looking for some single item to blame for the disaster that was his life. "I keeps telling myself I's going to give them up. And every time I's ready to, I gets sent back to one of them nuthouses and I's so bored and uptight I's got to keep using shit if I doesn't want to lose my mind."

Then Death struck home. Overdose. His favorite brother. O.D.'d on heroin. They'd found him on a rooftop, the works still hanging out of his arm. So Shadow went home again. Stone'cold sober this time.

He stood beside the coffin and cried and cried and called his brother's name and collapsed in the arms of his mother. And when he did go out to the streets again, they were different; no, he felt different. The fog was clearing, a kind of strength returning, or perhaps, welling up for the first time.

He was still Shadow. But a different Shadow. He would still need something in his head to fight the "hawk," but never again those drugs that murdered his brother.

"I's off drugs," he told me proudly. "I decided drinking is safer. It makes me just as happy. It's easier to get. Cheaper. Less cop troubles. You doesn't O.D. on it."

He was descending the five flights from my apartment to the street at the time. He was slightly inebriated and missed three steps, then clutching the rail, he pulled himself together. "One of these days when my life get better, I's going to stop drinking so much."

2
Randy

Randy was a delicate young man, thin and pale with a long face, the beginnings of a beard, and shoulder-length blond hair he was constantly tossing out of eyes as blue as the sky.

Adopted when but five months old, he never knew his real parents; and, since the couple who took him in had no children of their own, he was raised as an only child.

"Daddy" was a successful Kentucky moonshiner, a big shot in the Ku Klux Klan with excellent political connections. He had hoped Randy would choose a respectable career, perhaps become a junior partner in his own prosperous business.

Randy, however, wants nothing whatsoever to do with capitalism, which he rejects as the curse causing most of the world's ills. And, characteristically, Randy joined a Neo-Nazi party when he was barely twelve years old, because he felt they were out to change the world for the better. But as he grew a little older, he decided they weren't exactly "where it's at."

"Some of their ideas seemed a little far out," he recalls. "And when I learned more about what the Nazis did in Germany, I definitely made up my mind there must be a better way to change the world."

So he became a radical revolutionary. He started going to demonstrations, reading theoretical manuals, studying how to make explosives and listening devices and handle machine guns and other small arms.

About that time, his parents divorced and sent him to a military academy. He hated the discipline, but he set himself to learning all he could about any subject that might turn him into a competent revolutionary. He had actually become convinced that the only hope for a decent America was revolution by any means possible, a feeling shared by many young people.

He ran away from the academy as soon as he felt he had learned the basics. He was ready to take on the Establishment.

He hitched a ride to the nearest big town, where he hung around the hippiest section until he met some street people who told him where he could get a ride to New York, the biggest of the big cities, a wonderland of lights and dreams and, of course, the Empire State building and Times Square. Randy later described his path to New York as following the 'underground railroad' run by an informal group of people who sympathized with runaways, many of them former runaways themselves who not only arranged for stopovers and secret cars that took you where you wanted to go, but introduced you to the best location there for survival.

At that time Haight-Ashbury and the East Village were meccas for runaway flower children, seeking refuge in an alternative culture wherein Timothy Leary was the psychedelic guru and rock bands the angels of sound and fantastic light. They were joined by blacks on rebound from the Civil-Rights movement of the early sixties moving toward "Black· is beautiful," and black power. Whites and blacks merged into a psychedelic phase of diggers, hippies, crazies. They were searching, reaching out, withdrawing, gaining ground, losing their minds, deranging their senses, laughing at Lyndon Johnson, mourning the Kennedys and Martin Luther King, grooving on the contradictions within the society; turning on, tuning in, dropping out, returning, graduating to sex and religion, dancing in the new Age of Aquarius.

At St. Mark's Place the Electric Circus was in full swing, and a few blocks away the Filmore East, the mecca of rock. Panhandlers cruised about with flowers in their hair, their faces wreathed in smiles, promising peace and love.

Randy was fending for himself in the neon jungle, where stray boys are easy pickings for pimps and chicken hawks.

"I had a hard time at first. I met several older men who acted hip and offered me a place to spend the nght, then almost raped me when they got me home. It was one hassle after another.

"I guess I was really lucky, though. There's nothing like a little political consciousness. It keeps you on the right track. Some of the kids I met told me of horrible things they'd gone through.

"One kid told me that when he'd first run away he was picked up by some men at Port Authority who offered him a place to stay, and then when they got him home, stripped him naked, tied him to the bed, did all sorts of awful things to him, and took photos which they sold to S & M magazines."

Newsweek magazine wrote of a fifteen-year-old runaway picked up by an older man who gave him injections of the female hormone estrogen until he developed large breasts. In a way Randy was very lucky indeed to have been spared that fate, although he did have his share of "hassles," as he described them.

In 1971, three months after Randy came to New York, he wandered into the theater where a play of my old man's was being produced. He dug the scene and started hanging around there. The two of them became friends, and when my old man learned Randy didn't have a place to stay, he invited him to live with us.

Randy was a quiet, pleasant boy who spent most of his time studying revolutionary tactics out of books, and writing notes on how to start your own revolution.

He had some unique, but ultra-strong convictions about health and ecology. And, even though he had a revolutionary anti-religious outlook, he was afraid that the story of Adam and Eve just might be true and refused to eat or touch an apple or anything with apples in it.

He felt that people should not eat anything that was not openly given to them by Nature. For example, it was okay to eat oranges because they dropped off the trees and waited for men to pick them up. It was wrong to eat salt because it was not freely available to man, who had to dig into the earth or disturb sea water to obtain it. He subsisted solely on orange juice and plain white rice, which he was convinced contained all the vitamins and minerals necessary for a healthy existence. He refused to wear furs or leather in his belief that it was the ultimate sin to kill animals just to clothe ourselves when there were other materials that could replace their skins.

Randy watched every news show he could catch on TV and read all the available newspapers in order to keep up with current events all over the world so that he'd be all the better prepared when the time came to put his revolutionary techniques into practice. He loved science fiction; it expanded his mind and gave him new and better ideas that broadened his vision.

After he had spent several months with us, Randy phoned his father and gave him his address. His father begged him to return home. Randy made several short visits, but he always returned to New York as soon as he could, feeling uncomfortable with a father whose political ideas were the exact opposite of his own.

Although he considers communism preferable to capitalism, since it provides that no one goes hungry, homeless, or without medical care, he feels that the ideal society would be anarchistic, a world-sized Buddhist monastary where everyone meditates on the wonders of existence and produces only as much as is needed for survival.

"I'd like to see a revolution carried out by 80 or 90 percent of the population. A real people's revolution where we get the kind of world we'd like to have."

Last summer when my friend Jenny, my four-year-old son Raphael, and I went to California for a month, I left Randy in charge of my apartment on the lower East Side. By this time he had been staying with, off and on, for the last three years.

I returned to find that Randy had turned my place into a crash pad for Karen and Valerie, two young runaways he had met in my absence.

Now, a runaway is by definition a fugitive and it's risky business harboring one, let alone two. Should the police catch anyone sheltering a runaway, they have the legal right to make an arrest. I was tempted to ask the two girls to move out immediately. But they began recounting the terrible misfortunes they had suffered since leaving home and I simply could not throw them out on the streets. I suggested they telephone their parents. But then, when I saw their reactions and heard their descriptions of their respective home lives, I couldn't bring myself to give them the ultimatum of most halfway houses: Contact your nearest relative or get out!

Karen was an attractive fourteen-year-old with huge baby blue eyes, a small pouting mouth, long and straight honey-colored hair, and a fine woman's figure emerging from her adolescent baby fat. Both her parents were dead and she'd been living with her aunt for about a year "taking horrors you can't imagine." This aunt had four children of her own and was too busy for Karen, whom she looked upon as an unwanted burden.

Karen's friend Valerie, with her short blond hair, bright blue eyes, and effervescent smile, looked to me exactly like Sandra Dee. Every time I spoke to her, I felt I was taking part in a movie, a real Hollywood heartbreak drama of kids versus parents and the inclemencies of the street.

Valerie had been living with her father and mother. "But they can't even get along with each other. And neither of them digs me. Last time I ran away, they swore if I ever did it again they'd take it on themselves to see I spent the rest of my life behind bars." But not even that heavy threat could keep Valerie at home. Like countless thousands, she kept hearing the call of the wild and running off to answer it.

But, once away from familiar grazing grounds, life takes on hard edges, and the thin line between sincerity and guile explodes like a balloon in the faces of the naive, the trusting, the recklessly optimistic; upon those who, in a weird dance of hate, escape parental hardness and sterility to accept the first smile and the first ride until suddenly they find themselves at the edge of hell.

On one of their first nights in New York, Karen and Valerie were offered a ride by some well-dressed, hip-looking, flower-talking people. With their acceptance, they began that long journey into other worlds where they would harken to other voices lamoring for flesh gropings and mind freakings.

They were taken to a plush apartment in Queens and offered the world if they'd become prostitutes. Until then, neither of them had ever even talked to a prostitute in person; they had no idea what the life might be like. But the men promised them fancy wardrobes, their own luxurious apartments to work out of, and more money than they'd ever seen in their young lives.

Of course, Karen and Valerie were both very much concerned about finances. They had left home with little money and only the clothing they wore on their backs. "We'd never have got away from home," Valerie reminisced, "with Mom's Samsonite." So they were bare, easy pickings for the experienced eye.

At first the offer was tempting. After all, the people making it were exquisitely dressed and their spacious apartment dazzlingly set up with expensive furniture, satin bedspreads, fancy bars, and an expanse of thick white carpeting that seemed to swallow up their fears and misgivings. But neither of them really trusted these over-friendly strangers.

"We do need the money," Valerie said, "but I'm not sure I dig the idea."

"I think I'd like to go back to Manhattan," Karen said. At that point, two of the men forcefully escorted Valerie out of the room. "Hey, wait a minute," she yelled. "Where are you taking me?"

"We just want to talk to you for a few minutes," they told her.

"Can't we talk here - I want to stay with Karen."

"You'll be right back."

She was hitting and kicking as they dragged her out. Karen started after her, but a tall man in a mod suit grabbed her. "Get down on your hands and knees and swear you'll do anything I tell you to," the man told Karen.

She refused. He hit her. Hit hit her again and again. "He was actually beating me." She wished the carpet would open up and take her away, hide her; but there was no easy exit. Time and space slipped away; she felt only his blows and her tears. Then he was upon her, tearing her apart. She stopped struggling. He entered her with a rage. She threw him off and dashed for the door, but a prostitute guarded it.

Karen was terrified. "I want to see Valerie," she sobbed.

"You'll see Valerie when you do what I tell you. Now, get down on your knees!" He was swinging a belt, advancing on her. Still she refused. Her determination stabbed at him like a jagged rock, and he began to hit her again. By now her body was covered with bruises and she was hysterical. He stopped and tried to kiss her. She pushed him off.

She kept begging to be allowed to see her friend, but the pimp refused to let her see anyone until she agreed to join his stable. "But I was one tough cookie," as the pimp discovered.

He kept her a prisoner in his apartment for several days. She was numb with fear. "Each time he'd mention prostitution I'd freak out and he'd beat me up and rape me again. I hope to God I never have to go through anything like that again in my life."

Both Karen and Valerie were forcibly given injections of some type of hard drug-they think it was heroin-which increased the nightmarish aspects of the entire drama. Obviously it was meant to initiate an addiction that would push them into selling their bodies to pay for the habit.

As it was, Valerie already had a serious problem. She'd been raped the very first time she ran away while she and Karen were hitchhiking. And she had become pregnant in her Fallopian tubes. It had almost killed her. The tubes had burst from the pressure of the pregnancy and only an emergency operation had saved her life. The doctors had warned, no sex for at least six weeks for fear of serious complications. "Look," she said one day, casually raising her sweater to expose the huge scar on her stomach, a devil-may-care smile playing at the corner of her lips.

One day Karen's captors left her alone and she managed to climb down the fire escape and get away. When she returned to my apartment (this had all happened while I was on my way to Haight-Ashbury to check out the scene there), Karen learned that Valerie was still being held prisoner by the people who had picked them up. One time Valerie would call the apartment saying she was doing fine, just waiting until she'd completely recovered from her operation so she could make a lot of money. Then she'd call saying she wanted to leave, but they were holding her against her will. She would cry over the phone and beg Karen and Randy to help her escape. And just when Karen and Randy would make plans to rescue her, she would call back to say that she didn't want to leave yet, that she would wait until she'd gotten some money together. It was always money, and they began to dread the calls, although they looked forward to them as the only sign they had that she was still alive.

Then one day, after another desperate call from Valerie, Karen and Randy gathered together some friends, and took a cab to the expensive hotel in midtown Manhattan where Valerie was supposedly being held against her will. Valerie seemed overjoyed to see them, and they all left together without any resistance.

She was happy, ecstatic. She told everyone the pimps had tried to force her into prostitution. They had kept her drugged and locked in a room. She was so relieved to be back, to be free. But there were lingering residues of the nightmare. She kept talking about how the pimp owed her one hundred dollars. I never understood exactly why he owed her the money as she was still recovering from her operation and was still not permitted to have sex. Apparently she wasn't leveling with us.

Valerie became more and more restless. She had only the clothes the pimp had given her and was completely broke. I was buying food for all of us, but couldn't afford to give the girls an allowance. It really bothered her, that she was so broke while someone owed her one hundred dollars. Neither Karen nor Valerie had ever had to worry about money for basic necessities before, and although Karen had adjusted to it gracefully, Valerie found poverty a dreadful bore.

"If only my scar would heal," she'd say, "I'd be able to make some money. I can't stand begging for pennies and I'm sick of wearing the same clothes every day. If only we could have brought along a bag with some clean clothes, or if we could risk going home to pick up some clothes."

Although she wouldn't dare return to her parents for clothes, Valerie would endanger her life daily. Every time she went into the streets, she'd run into a pimp she'd met through the people who'd first picked her up. Each time the pimp would come up with a new story and Valerie would go along with him, wide-eyed, believing that this one was different. And Karen was constantly jeopardizing her own safety going to rescue her best friend, who kept getting into one scrape after another and calling the apartment for help. I never did get to know Valerie very well. She was in and out of the apartment, never really seemed at home there, and always appeared hesitant to discuss her situation.

Karen was more open, searching for answers, analyzing. "No matter what I do," she complained, "I can't seem to please my aunt. She just doesn't like me." Karen had grown up poor. And, worse than that, she had grown up a poor relative, the only daughter of an early widowed mother, whose aunt, uncle, and cousins lived the way the people in TV ads live.

Karen's father had died when she was three. Her mother supported herself and her young daughter mostly by waiting on tables. She changed jobs often and never had any financial security. Often she was unable to get a baby-sitter. When Karen was four and five, her mother began to leave her at home by herself while she worked. Her mother was always tired when she came home from work and often slept through most of her hours at home. So, as a young child, Karen was left on her own a good deal of the time.

Karen's mother, feeling guilty because she couldn't give Karen the attention or the material goods she felt the child should have, would send

Karen to spend weekends with her prosperous married sister. This sister thoroughly disapproved of Karen's mother and made no effort to conceal her disapproval from the child. The aunt and uncle had four children of their own who ranged in age from Karen's age to almost ten years older.

Karen's relationship with her mother was a stormy one, clouded by her mother's regrets that she could do no better for herself and her child and her fears that her young daughter would become as worn and embittered by life as she had become.

Then when Karen was twelve, the mother became ill. With a premonition that she had not much life left in her, she planned a trip to New York with her young daughter. Karen later described this trip with her mother as the happiest time of her life. The two of them went on a spree, mostly in the East Village where my apartment was located, which must have had heavy overtones for Karen.

"We were like sisters. We went everywhere together. After so many years of never having time for me, Mother tried to crowd a whole lifetime of living together into those short months.

"But even though I didn't know she was dying then, she knew it and it was like a heavy cloud hanging over us. I could sense something was wrong even though she refused to admit it."

When they returned home, the mother's life was ebbing, while the daughter had gleaned a vision of what life might be like for her.

Karen's mother died soon after the trip in a haze of mutual re-criminations and unexpressed affection. Karen went to live with her well-to-do aunt, the same one who had condescended to Karen and her mother all of Karen's life. The aunt was surprised when Karen didn't adjust to a "normal family life," didn't avidly follow the examples of her virtuous cousins. Instead she befriended the longhairs, the pot smokers in her high school, those who had had brushes with the law. The aunt was shaken by Karen's lack of "ambition," her failure to look like a proper young lady, and most of all, by her frank sexual interest in young men and her friendship with Valerie, whom she considered wild.

Finally Karen got sick of the scoldings and the daily reminders that she was no good like her mother. She and Valerie set out for the big city.

They had nowhere to go, and nothing to do except survive. They were on the make. They hung out in parks, began relationships with men that were quickly consummated and abruptly discontinued. Karen felt ambivalent about the numerous men she had made it with. She was not sexually attracted to most of them, but motivated instead by her conviction that her body was the only coin she had to offer for food, for shelter, for even a few moments of attention.

So there they were, these two experienced and rather tragic young ladies staying with me.

One Saturday evening, Karen told me she was going across the street to visit some mutual friends of ours. Valerie had gone out earlier, but she had a habit of staying away for several days at a time so I gave no thought to her absence. Karen, however, was usually home by nine or ten, so when midnight arrived without a word from her I started to wonder. Then the phone rang. "It's the police," Randy said. "They want to speak to you, Maryanne." I got up from the desk where Jenny and I had been collating our notes on runaways in California.

"Mrs. Raphael?" the voice asked. "This is the police. We'd like to ask you a few questions. Do you know a Karen Hayes?"

"Karen Hayes?" I said, realizing only then that I'd never asked Karen her last name.

I asked Randy. He shrugged his shoulders.

"I'm not sure," I told the police. "I know a Karen, but I don't know her last name."

"Then she's not your sister?" he asked. "She says she's your sister."

I didn't know what to say without making things worse for Karen.

"Do you know how old she is?" he asked.

"No," I said truthfully for at that time I didn't know her exact age.

"What do you know about her?" he asked angrily.

"Not much. She started living at my apartment while I was out of town. I came home and found her here. I didn't know how old she was and we didn't have much chance to talk about anything."

"Haven't you ever heard it's against the law to harbor a fugitive?" he asked, getting even angrier.

"I didn't know she was a fugitive," I said. "What is she wanted for?"

He ignored my question, gave me a little lecture on the law against harboring a fugitive, which he said was punishable by imprisonment, then hung up. When I put the phone down, I told Randy the police had arrested Karen and they might be coming by the house, so we should make sure there was nothing in the apartment to get us into any more trouble.

"Do you really think the police will come here?" Randy asked.

"They very well might," I said. "Do you have anything you don't want them to see?"

"Definitely," Randy said.

"Well, you'd better hurry and get it out of here," I told him.

"I'll need help," Randy said.

"Help? What in the world do you have here?"

"My homemade bombs, the list of all the revolutionaries, all my revolutionary equipment, plans for making an atomic bomb."

I couldn't tell whether he was serious or joking. But I wasn't taking any chances.

"Get the bombs out immediately,"I said, ready to have an instant nervous breakdown at the idea that there could have been bombs in my apartment. "And if you have any grass, get it out, too!"

I went into the living room where I'd left Jenny and asked if she'd help Randy get some things out of the house. Without asking what the bags contained, she helped him carry them to a nearby apartment where a friend lived. While they were gone, I called Jason, a friend of ours who lives in Brooklyn, a 275-pound Italian who's had lots of dealing with the police and so far has always come out ahead. I asked him to come right over.

When Jenny and Randy returned, we cleaned out the apartment to make sure there were no homemade bombs or hand grenades left under a sofa or in a corner somewhere. Then Jenny suggested we all go to her place to work on the runaway notes, our plan for the evening before that call.

"I want to stay here and answer the phone if it rings," Randy said. "Karen may be calling. When you're arrested you do get one call."

"Okay," I said. "When Jason comes you can tell him what's been happening. I didn't want to talk over the phone. And tell him we're at Jenny's."

Jenny and I got our kids dressed and walked a few blocks to her apartment. I called Randy to check on things. Jason answered the phone. His voice was calm. "The police are here now," he said. "They've arrested Karen and she told them she and Valerie were both staying here. So they're waiting for Valerie."

"When everything's finished at my apartment," I told Jason, "Come over. And bring me some tranquilizers. I'm a nervous wreck. I'm afraid I'll be in trouble, too."

"You're in no trouble," Jason said. "You could have been. Karen told the police you knew she was a runaway and you were writing a book on runaways and had asked to interview her.

"They said they could arrest you for harboring a runaway; but they promised not to press charges so don't worry. I'll be over as soon as they leave, but it may be a long time because they're waiting for Valerie to return."

"Well, anyhow, come as soon as it's all over," I told him.

Several hours later, Jenny's doorbell rang. I was certain it was the police and was relieved to see Jason and Randy alone.

"Did Valerie finally arrive?"

"No," Jason said, "She called. I tried to warn her not to come over; but the cops were listening to everything I said.

"I did manage to get them out of the house by telling them that Valerie sometimes stays out all night and that there was a good chance she wouldn't be coming home. As soon as they left, we left the house."

We tried to think of a way to get in touch with Valerie and warn her of the situation, but none of us knew where she spent her time. Around four A.M., Jason went home. Randy, Raphael, and I spent the rest of the night at Jenny's.

The next morning, Randy and I stopped at the small grocery store just outside our apartment building. The young Puerto Rican clerk said, "Did you know the police arrested your little friend this morning?"

So they had arrested Valerie.

"What happened?"

"Well, the little blond girl was in here buying some beer when two policemen and a policewoman walked up to her and told her she was under arrest.

"They took her away. She kept asking them why they were arresting her, but they wouldn't say."

Several days passed with no word concerning the girls' fate. Randy was wild-eyed, restless, making all sorts of outrageous plans to rescue them from wherever they were being held prisoners. He'd sit nervously by the phone waiting for the girls to call. Or, he'd make one call after the other to lawyers, runaway half-way houses, any place he could think of that might give him any kind of information.

Finally the long-expected call from Karen came. She was in a detention home, waiting to go on trial. She said Valerie was in an even worse detention home, with little chance of getting out until she's eighteen. Randy was really desperate after the call. He felt we should all get together and save them, but nobody could come up with a workable plan.

Jason suggested I call Karen's aunt and see what her plans were. "Maybe there's some way we can soften her up. She might even agree to let you have Karen live here if you could convince her you're reliable and respectable.

"Tell her you're a social worker. Give her all your credentials."

"The aunt knows Karen was staying here," I said. "I'm sure she won't trust me now. She might even press charges against me for helping Karen run away."

"The police already said they weren't going to arrest you," Jason replied.

Randy looked at me with a mixture of hope and threat, as though it was my responsibility to save Karen.

"Those were New York policemen who said they wouldn't arrest me for harboring runaways," I reminded him. "But Karen's from New Jersey and that's where her aunt lives. She could call the New Jersey police and they haven't given me any promises."

"You're just being paranoid," Jason said.

"Why don't you call Karen's aunt?" I said.

"That's absolutely out," Jason said. "If you think you could get in trouble for letting Karen stay here, think what trouble I'd be in if they found out I'd made it with her. I could go to jail for a long time.

"She's only fourteen. That's statutory rape. And I can't tell what Karen would say under stress. She got so upset when she was arrested she told the cops she'd been staying here and she even told them about Valerie. I can't afford to take any chances.

"Karen evidently made it with about thirty guys during the three weeks she was in New York. I realized after awhile it was because she doesn't think she has anything else to offer.

"I took her to my farm. Nobody made a pass at her all day and she spent most of the time apologizing for her existence.

"I'll do anything I can for Karen. If you work out something with the aunt so that she can stay here, I'll give her some money to live on. But I can't take any risks that might involve me with her."

Randy was looking completely disillusioned. He was becoming convinced that the entire adult world, represented by Jason, Jenny, and me as well as the aunt and the police, were in collusion against him and his two friends, that any apparent interest in getting Karen released was simply an attempt to pacify him.

"Maybe you should call the aunt," Jason said, turning to Jenny. "Feel her out. See how she'd feel about Karen's staying with Maryanne."

So Jenny called Karen's aunt in rural New Jersey. She introduced herself as Maryanne Raphael in whose home Karen had lived, because she felt it was a good way to find out how the aunt felt about me. The aunt immediately went into a harangue about how Karen had always been a problem. She bewailed Karen's inadequacies, her lying, her carelessness, her lack of gratitude. She blamed it on the undisciplined life Karen had led with her mother. As the conversation wore on, she began to vilify Karen more and more until any veneer of a modern, rational, psychologically oriented attitude toward Karen's problems vanished and what lay exposed was the aunt's passionate hatred of Karen's sexuality, a hard-lined puritanical vengefulness that Jenny had never seen equalled.

"I don't understand it," the aunt said. "We give Karen everything. We try to make a good life for her. And what does she do? Instead of making friends with decent kids, she finds all the misfits, all the drug users, all the kids who've been in trouble with the law. Those were Karen's friends. Like that Valerie she went to New York with. She's a little whore."

Jenny couldn't get a word in.

"Karen even has her own horse. We bought it for her. But she neglects it. She won't exercise it.

"And there's Karen's wardrobe. She asked me for a whole lot of clothes. I bought her everything she wanted. So what does she wear? The same pair of dirty, holey blue jeans day after day.

"You can see her legs and her underpants. It's not decent.

"And the way she lets all the boys know she's available. When Karen used to go to the pool with my daughter, my daughter was embarrassed by Karen. Karen would throw herself at all the lifeguards. My daughter said to me, 'Mother, I don't want to go swimming with Karen any more. It's disgusting the way she acts.'

"And I'm sure she's been doing the same thing in New York. That's why she's in a detention home. And that's where she'll stay. She doesn't know how to act around decent folks. Just like her mother. I thought we could change her, but she's beyond help.

"She's no good."

After that, what could Jenny say? The aunt's tone of voice had made it evident she was more interested in punishing Karen for her transgressions of the aunt's moral codes than in helping the young girl. Jenny didn't dare suggest the possibility of Karen's coming to live with us. Karen would have wanted that and what kind of punishment would that have been?

So where was the solution? What could be done for Karen?

Randy talked about marrying Karen or Valerie, thinking it would be possible to make one of them an "emancipated minor," no longer subject to their relatives' guardianship. "I'll marry the first one who escapes," he said.

He wrote long letters to Karen in the detention home. None of us had Valerie's address. In Randy's letters, he spoke about springing Karen from the institution with the use of firearms or explosives. He wrote in code but the code was decipherable enough to get his point across. The torture of adults was driving him crazy. Eventually, we got a letter from the detention home telling us that it was a waste of time and stamps to continue writing her as the rules of the home did not allow the girls to receive mail from anyone other than parents or guardians.

Randy had learned that when the police picked up Karen she was covered with bruises. She had been with the pimps from Queens again just prior to the arrest. He was determined to avenge this. He tried to round up friends to go with him in search of the pimps.

"If the girls were still in danger," Jason told Randy, "I'd be willing to go and rescue them as I did once before. But I won't risk trouble just for revenge. How would it help Karen or Valerie?"

"It might not help Karen or Valerie," Randy said, "but it might help other young girls. It might make those punks think twice before they attack other runaways."

"There are too many pimps in New York to teach them all a lesson," Jason told Randy, "and if we did scare these two, there'd still be a whole city full of them out there."

"We should form an organization to protect runaways," Randy said, very earnestly.

"The police are supposed to do that," Jason told him.

"The police?" Randy said. "Who did the police arrest? Karen and Valerie. They're in jail while the men who tortured them are free, on the loose ready to attack some other girls.

"Even if the police really tried to protect them, the kids would be afraid to go to the police for protection. Right now, of course, it's against the law to run away, so runaways can't go to the police for protection.

"But even if they changed the law, which they'd do if they really cared at all bout the kids, runaways still wouldn't go to the cops because the cops are against all young people. They see us as potential or actual revolutionaries.

"They see every young kid as a threat to the Establishment. So where do they think the future of the Establishment will come from?"

We agreed with many of Randy's statements. The law that makes running away a crime in itself often does more harm than good. It makes runaways fugitives from the law, removes all the protection the law could otherwise offer them, and often forces them to turn to people who are already outside the law for help. Thus young runaways are easy prey ato many criminals who feel certain they can exploit them in almost any way they wish. How can the young people report them to the police?

We knew, too, that Randy was right about how youth did not trust the police because the police saw young people as potential troublemakers. Everything possible should be done to establish better relationships between youngsters and the police. This is of major importance if the next generation is to have any kind of respect for our country's laws. Some of these laws should be changed immediately, and the enforcement of others tempered with realism and mercy so as to better reflect our changing times and the anguish of our children, searching for equality in a world they're about to inherit.

In many states, the law against "running away" makes it a crime for anyone under eighteen to stay away from home more than twenty-four hours without the permission of his or her parent or guardian. Actually, this law discriminates against youth since the parent or guardian can stay away from home for as long as he or she wishes without having committed a crime. Witness the growing number of divorces. Maybe we should require the children's permission before parents can divorce?

I could have been arrested for harboring fugitives just because I couldn't bear to send those two girls back home, where I felt they'd run away again and probably end up in another dangerous situation. Of course, I was unable to give them the guidance they needed. If running away and harboring runaways had not been against the law, I might have been able to lead these youngsters to people who might have been able to help them work out their problems and find a better place in the sun.

How could we start an organization to help runaways? None of us hae the time or the money. Jenny and I told Randy we hoped our book might attract our society's interest and involvement, as well as help youngsters and their parents work out solutions so that running away would be unnecessary or at least not so traumatic for all concerned.

The Runaway Child Act, which would provide $10 million a year for three years for shelter and guidance of young runaways, would be a step in the right direction. But it's still stalled in the House of Representatives while one million teen-agers continue to disappear from home every year, all too many of them falling into the hands of pimps like those who tortured Karen and Valerie, or some equally obnoxious characters.

Karen was finally released in her aunt's custody, against the aunt's expressed wishes. Her aunt felt Karen should be imprisoned to teach her a lesson. But the judge felt reform school would do Karen more harm than good and told the aunt she had no choice in the matter. At least, that's what Karen told us when she was able to call during her lunch hour from school. She warned us we shouldn't call her at her aunt's, since her aunt had told her she was not to contact any of her outside friends.

And Valerie? From Karen's reports, she is still in the reform school, but is signing up with a job-training program. Thereafter, she will live in some sort of dormitory arrangement and have access to the street during the daytime.

We recently received a letter from Karen:

Hi everybody,

How are you? I'm ok. I'm in school now. Ha. It sucks. My aunt is being a real drag. You would think that she would let me have some freedom cause I'm not going to be here for long (thank God) but she's not letting me out or anything. If I make one slip, I go back to the detention home. I swear she hates. me.

People are so fucked up here. It seems that they're trying to please one another instead of pleasing themselves. I wore the sparkle shirt Maryanne gave me with blue dungarees and bright red platform shoes, and you should have seen the dirty looks I got.

Some girl goes, "what are you doing with that shirt?" I said, I'm wearing it, and she said, "you dig that stuff?" And I said yes, and then she said, "Well, maybe I don't dig you." All I said was, "I didn't ask you to dig me, so mind your own business."

I'm going to talk to my probation officer and see if Jenny could get custody of me. My P.O. and psychiatrist and the judge are on my side. So my aunt has no say in the matter on me cause I'm in the state's custody.

What's happening with you? Tell everybody I send my love.

Karen

One month after Karen and Valerie were arrested, I came home one night to find Randy sitting on the couch, his arms around a young, pretty girl. I called him into the kitchen so I could speak to him privately.

"Is she a runaway?"

"Oh, no," he assured me. "She's over eighteen. She showed me her driver's license."

"Well, I'm glad we won't be accused of harboring a runaway this time."

"I met Judy at Contact," Randy said. "I had gone there to meet a friend. Judy had just come in from New Jersey, and was hoping they'd find her a place to stay. We liked each other right away, so I told her she could stay here if you agreed."

She was petite. She had soft black hair and large, dark, expressive eyes. She was quiet and demure, and seemed shy with everyone except Randy and my four-year-old son. She and Randy spent most of their time with their arms around each other, engrossed in intimate conversation.

So Judy became a member of the household.

Late one evening, Randy and Judy returned from an outing. Both appeared disturbed.

"We went to see Judy's uncle," Randy said. "He lives in a big apartment in the seventies, somewhere on the west side. He told us Judy's father had been in touch with the runaway squad here in New York."

"I thought you said you were eighteen." I couldn't believe we had another runaway on our hands.

They both blushed.

"My father told the police I was fourteen," Judy said. "So they'll be looking for me."

"Then I guess you won't be able to stay here," I said. "Ever since the Runaway Squad found Karen and Valerie here, they've been pulling midnight raids on us."

It was true. The police had come once at midnight, once at five A.M. and once at three o'clock in the afternoon. They came inside and looked in every room, obviously searching for bodies for they only looked in places large enough for a person to hide, on top of the loft bed, under the regular bed, in the closets, in the bathroom.

Although Randy had been there each time they came, they assumed he belonged until the third visit when they began questioning him.

"What's your name? How old are you?"

I had told them his parents knew he was staying here and had given their permission. But they ordered him to go along with them to the station, where they kept him until they had phoned his father and verified the information that Randy and I had given them.

"My father could really cause a lot of trouble," Judy said. "I mean, he's really a nasty guy."

"But your uncle seemed pretty friendly," said Randy, turning to Judy.

"Yes," Judy said brightly. "He said he'd help us."

Her expression remained troubled, in contrast to the enthusiasm in her voice.

The two went into the kitchen. I assumed they were going to have a late snack, and was surprised when they emerged half an hour later with a suitcase and a plastic bag full of peanut-butter-and-jelly sandwiches (the only time I ever saw Randy go off his orange and rice diet). They informed me they were going into hiding.

"We don't want to cause you any trouble," Randy said, "so we're not even going to tell you where we'll be."

I had a hunch they'd be at our friend Lou's place a few blocks away, which turned out to be true. But their departure had been so dramatic, so definitive, that I was a bit disconcerted when the "fugitives," holding hands as usual, returned the next afternoon for more provisions.

Two days later, Randy called to say everything was all right, and I was surprised when he came by the following night with a large bruise on his face and a black-and-blue mark under the left eye. Before I could ask him what had happened, he poured out the story.

"Judy and I went to her uncle's house again because Judy needed some more money. I don't know if he set us up or what, but after we'd been there a short time, Judy's father came storming in.

"The uncle tried to calm him down. He sat in a chair instead of attacking us, which is what it looked like he wanted to do.

"He kept on trying to intimidate me. He made jokes like 'Do you know why Sicilians wear pointed shoes? So we can kill roaches in corners', all the time glaring at me like I was a roach.

"He made a lot of vague threats such as 'Don't worry, you'll be taken care of.'

"Judy told her father we were in love and wanted to be together. Her father pretended to agree to this. He suggested we take a ride with him and discuss it.

"As soon as we were outside the uncle's apartment, her father became much harsher.

"He glared at me all the way down in the elevator.

"When we were in the lobby, he turned toward me, 'You bastard!' he growled and laid a heavy right into my eye and two or three more blows to my body.

"After that he backed away. His hand was still raised like he wanted to hit me some more, but was holding back for some reason.

"Before he left, he pointed his finger at me and shouted, 'If she's pregnant, I'll kill you!'

"I was so scared I just wandered the streets not really knowing where I was. I had this feeling I was being followed.

"Somehow I ended up at this taxi garage. I called Jenny and asked to pick me up in her car. She said the car wasn't near her house and besides since I was in a taxi garage why didn't I take a cab and she'd pay for it when I got to her house.

"I stayed at Jenny's all day today because I was too paranoid to come back here.

"Jenny finally convinced me that Judy's father wouldn't be able to tell in a day's time whether his daughter was pregnant."

Finally Randy paused for breath. He began to relax a little. His face brightened.

"Hey, I never showed you Karen's letter. Did I?"

Hi Randy,

Been "home" for a week now. I ain't really free, but it's an improvement.

As for my aunt, if there's any way she can bug me she does. I wish that woman had something to live for besides getting on my case.

She had to let me out of the house to go to school. Freedom to go from one prison to the next! Ha.

Right now I'm in hot water again. My aunt feels I take too long to get home from school. She keeps threatening to send me back to the detention home.

Do you think Maryanne or Jenny will be able to do anything about getting custody of me? I really need a place where I can breathe. I miss all of you and hope to join you in the real world one of these days. Life in creepsville is a bitch.

Love & kisses,

Karen

If Randy had been upset after Karen and Valerie's arrest, he was dazed after Judy's father took her back home.

"I don't know what her father will do to her," he kept saying. "She told me he's always beating her up. He might kill her. You should have seen how mad he was. He's really crazy.

"I've got to rescue her," he kept saying, "I've got to. I've got to. And we can run off together, maybe to California."

At first Jason considered the possibility of driving Randy to New Jersey to Judy's house, but when Randy started making frantic phone calls trying to locate some rifles and machine guns, Jason decided it was too dangerous.

Randy was heartbroken. But then he got some good news. A friend of a friend was looking for an unmarried woman to marry her foreign boyfriend so he could stay in the country. She herself was waiting on a divorce from her first husband so she could marry again. But the boyfriend's situation was desperate and he couldn't afford to wait for her divorce. She would pay Judy one thousand dollars for being the stand-in bride. Randy quickly made the arrangments, promising to have Judy there for the following Wednesday morning for the wedding.

"That's perfect," he told us. "We'll rescue Judy on Tuesday. Wednesday morning she can marry the guy and we'll get the money and leave immediately for California.

Randy got his friends Lou and Lynn to go with him. Jenny told them they could use her car, the old Dodge we'd driven to California in, if they could get it to run.

Randy was worried because he had been unable to get hold of any guns. "Don't worry," Lou told him. "I know karate. I can handle the old man."

It was after midnight when they finally returned.

"Where's Judy?" I asked.

"She didn't want to come," Lynn said.

"What do you mean?" I asked. "She didn't want to come? Randy, didn't you check with Judy before you went to rescue her?"

Randy blushed. "It's not that she didn't want to come," he said. "She couldn't come. She's afraid of her father."

"She could have come," Lynn insisted. "She had a chance before her father came home."

"She was afraid," Randy said. "She really wants to come. She's still planning on it. But she wants to save some money first. And her father promised to buy her a car. She's waiting for the car, so we'll have something to travel in."

"But what about the thousand dollars" I asked Randy. "You guys could have taken that money and got away."

"I know," Randy said. "But Judy was really afraid. She's terrified of her father. She showed me bruises all over her arms where he beat her. She said she wants to wait for the best time."

"It was really wild," Lou said, reliving the abortive rescue. "After we left Judy's house and started home, this big car came zooming down the road and almost rammed right into us. It swirled at the last moment.

"We stopped to see what was happening and the car stopped. It was Judy's father and he had Judy next to him. She was huddled in the corner, looking terrified."

"Her father screamed at me," Randy said excitedly, "He wanted me to get out and fight him like a man. He had something in his hand. I think it was a gun. I thought he was going to kill me right then and there.

" 'This is my turf,' her father said, 'Do you think you can come on my turf and get away with it? Come on, get out of the car.'

" 'I'll get out of the car!' Lou shouted, and he jumped out before Judy's father knew what was happening. He was too eager to take the father on; so the father changed his mind. He must have decided Lou was dangerous."

"I am," Lou said. "I didn't give a damn if the old bastard had a gun. I would have got it away from him and killed him with his own weapon if he'd come after me. But he kept saying, 'I don't want to fight you. I've got nothing against you.'

"I told him I'm with Randy. You tackle Randy and you tackle me. Finally he got the message and split."

"As he drove away," Randy said, "he shouted, 'Randy, if I ever catch you in my territory again, you're dead. Wow! I'm still shaking. I really believe that man wants to kill me."

Randy and Judy continued their love affair through letters and occasional phone calls whenever Judy could get to a phone without her father's knowledge. About six months after the "rescue", Judy did manage to get away. She joined Randy and they called to tell us goodbye.

"We can't talk now. Judy's father is after us. So we haven't much time. We just wanted to tell you we're together and we're going somewhere where we can be free."

"Good luck," I told them. "Let me know how things work out."

"They've worked out," Judy said blissfully.

"We'll get in touch whenever we feel it's safe," Randy said. "But Judy's father doesn't play. He told her he'd kill both of us if she ran away again. That's why she was afraid to leave at first.

"What does he expect her to do? He makes it impossible for her to live at home and threatens to kill her if she leaves."

"Take care," I told them.

"We will," Randy said. "So long."

That was nine months ago. So far there's been no word from them. I hope wherever they are, those two kids have found someplace where they can be free to make a life for themselves.

As sometimes happens when you're writing, your characters seem to get the message that you're writing about them and suddenly pop back into your life. Well, in a way that's what happened with Randy. There was a phone call from his mother whom I'd never met.

"Maryanne, I want to thank you for all you did for Randy. He's told me so many wonderful things about you. And I wanted to know if you've heard from him recently. I'm very worried about him."

I told her how long it had been since I last saw him.

"Oh, I've seen him since then," she said disappointed. "He and Judy came home to my house a few months ago. They stayed with me awhile, then they'd stay awhile with Randy's father. We're divorced, you know.

"They were afraid all the time that Judy's father would find them. They told me some horrible stories about him.

"But a terrible thing happened before Randy left, and I'm afraid he thinks I'm mad at him. I was awfully mad at him, but I'm not any more. I'm just worried. But he's probably afraid to get in touch with me. If he calls you, or contacts anyone you know, please please give him the message that I'm not angry with him and that I'm worried and want to know he's okay."

She started crying then. "I hate to bother you with my problems.

"You've done so much for Randy. It was so awful. The last time he and Judy were here, they told me they had to leave because her father had somehow got our address.

"They asked me to drive them to a place in the highway where it was good to hitchhike. I had given them a little money, but I don't really have much. Randy's father has money, but I don't.

"Anyway, I did offer to drive them, and while we were in the car, Randy pointed to a place on the highway and said, 'This is fine. We'll get off here.'

"I stopped the car to let them out, and Randy pulled a knife on me. I couldn't believe it. He's always been such a gentle boy. But he did. He pulled a knife and said, 'We're not getting out here. You are. And leave your pocketbook.'

"I wanted to die. It was like a nightmare. I don't know how I did it, but I finally managed to talk them out of taking the car and my purse.

"I ended up driving them to the bus station and giving them some more money for tickets. But I don't know where they went.

"Randy broke my heart. But he is my son and I love him. And I'm worried about him. If you hear anything from him, please ask him to call me. Tell him I'm not mad. I love him."

3
Frances

Go West, young man! At a certain age, he sets out to seek his fortune. Sometimes with his parents' approval. Or, he runs away. As legend has it, the parents would actually tell the child: "It's time for you to go into the world and see how many dragons you can slay." et cetera.

But girls will also be girls, and since the rise of the feminist movement, more and more young women are deciding that they too have a right to adventure. Today more females than males are leaving home. They go because their parents either allow their brothers more freedom or expect their daughters to do too many household chores. Maybe they feel their movement is too restricted, or perhaps they simply want to be free, to taste the honey of their dreams.

Of course, there have always been women who ran away to get married or to try their luck at becoming a movie star or a singer, or even to join a circus. And today it's no different. There's still the lunge to make it the celluloid way.

For example, take Frances, young, white, from the Midwest, shy, eager, womanly before her full time, but letting nothing hold her back. Attractive with long, flowing brown hair and a well-developed body for what turns out at second glance to be a young girl.

I met her when she tried out for a part in a play by a friend of mine. Frances had already made a name for herself in underground movies as the star of several porno films that had found a large following among the avant-garde. My friend was ready to award her the part until he learned that she was only sixteen years old despite those large brown bedroom eyes and sensuous lips.

Frances and I became good friends and she managed to tell me a great deal of her life story. Like Shadow, she came from a poor family that had too many children and too little space to raise them in. But in addition to crowded conditions and poverty, Frances had the problem of being the oldest girl, which meant her parents expected her to become a sort of third parent to the younger children; to help care for them, share in the housework, the laundry, cooking, ironing, and so on.

"But what I hated the most about this," she told me, "was that I was blamed for any trouble they'd get into. If my little brother skipped school, I was the one who got a beating. If my little sister made a mess, I was the one who had to clean it up. 'You're the oldest,' Mother would always say. 'You should have been watching them.'

"It was a real drag. I never had a chance to be a kid. They forced me to grow up and be a surrogate mother at ten years old. 'It might not have been so bad if they had given me the freedoms and privileges that go along with being an adult. But my father was as strict with me as with any of the younger kids I was expected to take care of. 'If I wanted to go to a movie with one of the guys in my class, my dad would say I was too young. If I stayed out after nine o'clock when I went to visit a girl friend, he made me stay in for a week.

"Finally I just couldn't take any more. When I was almost fifteen, I knew I had to get away or I'd go crazy. So I started making plans to run away.

"Ever since I was a little girl I used to daydream about being a famous movie star. I wanted to live most of my life at night because the night was so much more exciting than the day. Of course, my parents would never allow me out at night, and they'd make me go to bed at ten every night and come in and turn off the light if they found me up reading movie magazines, love comics, or romantic novels, which happened every night since I'm a night person at heart and could never go to sleep before midnight.

"When my mom would take away my book or magazine and turn off the light, I'd lie there dreaming of the day when I'd come to the big city and be discovered by a famous movie director and become a popular actress and have handsome actors fighting for my attentions. I wanted to be surrounded all the time with beautiful, elegant people and never have to worry about money the way Mom and Dad did.

"I used to sit and plan what I'd ask for if my fairy godmother ever appeared and gave me four wishes and those were the ones I decided upon. I was very naive. I believed in fairy godmothers until I was ten. My friends used to tease me about it, but I insisted it was true. It had to be true. My life was so empty and I just knew that something wonderful had to come and change it."

Once Frances had accepted the fact that no fairy godmother or handsome prince on a white horse was coming to rescue her, she made up her mind to do something.

"We lived in a small town in Indiana. My father worked for the electric company and didn't make enough money to support six children, but my family were strict Catholics and didn't believe in birth control. So the kids kept coming.

"As I said before, my father expected me to be an adult when it came to taking care of the kids, but he'd never let me do anything I really wanted to do. So I had been making plans for a long time to run away.

"Then when I was a freshman in high school I tried out for cheerleader. Cheerleaders were elected by the entire high school. I didn't think I had a chance so I didn't even bother to tell my parents I was trying out.

"When I was elected I was so excited, so proud and happy. It was a chance to really have some fun, to go to ball games that were played out of town and to make a lot of new friends. I'd never had much social life so it looked like my golden opportunity.

"But the minute I told Mom and Dad, they said I couldn't do it. I wasn't allowed to stay out that late. They needed me at home after school to help with the kids and the housework. I promised to get up early every morning and to work on the weekends until I got all my work done, but no matter how I begged and pleaded, they said I couldn't be a cheerleader.

"That was the last straw, so I borrowed some money from my boyfriend Al. My parents didn't even know I had a boyfriend because they didn't allow me to go with boys; but from time to time when they thought I was with a girl friend, I would go out with Al.

"Of course, Al was in high school and didn't have much money himself. But he had enough to buy me a Greyhound bus ticket to New York, with enough left over for meals during the trip. I wanted to go to California since I was interested in becoming a movie star, but when I asked the price of a ticket to Hollywood, I knew it would take me ages to get that much money together."

The bus ride lasted twenty hours and although she had tried to stretch her money, after buying cokes, hot dogs, hamburgers, potato chips and candy bars, when she arrived at Port Authority she had only two dollars left.

"But I was so hungry I sat down on one of the stools at the terminal and ordered breakfast. I looked around me and couldn't believe all the people. I'd never seen so many people in my life. And there I was without any money; no friends, no place to go, no job and no experience.

"I was scared to death. If I'd had enough money I might have taken the next bus that headed west and gone home. But I had no choice. So I tried to calm myself as I ate. My hand was shaking so much I could barely drink my orange juice.

"Before I finished eating, two goodlooking young men sat down next to me. Both of them were tall and then with hair a little too long so that it fell on their foreheads. They were wearing stylish mod suits with tight pants. They looked so much alike I wondered if they were twins. They were talking about what plays were casting and which parts they wanted to try out for.

"I noticed they had a copy of *Variety* and I asked if I could borrow it.

" 'Sure thing,' they guy next to me said, 'but we have to have it back because there's some shows in there we want to try for.'

"I asked them if they knew of any parts I could try out for.

"They asked me if I was an actress and I told them I'd been in some school plays back in Indiana and everyone said I was very good.

"The two men looked at each other and smiled. 'There's a lot more competition in New York than there is in Indiana,' one of them said.

"I laughed. 'I don't intend to become a star overnight,' I told them. 'I'm willing to start at the bottom.'

" 'Baby, you don't know how low the bottom can be,' one of them said.

" 'Oh, I don't care. I'm willing to take any part, just so I'm acting.'

" 'Are you serious about that?'

" 'Very serious.'

"They told me they knew a film director who was always looking for actors.

"I became very excited and asked them for his name and address.

"They told me they'd take me to meet him, and asked if I wanted to go right then.

"They called a taxi. The three of us got inside. They introduced themselves as Theodore and Ned.

"I told them my name was Fifi and they said they liked it.

"I was disappointed to find out that the director lived in an ordinary brownstone in Brooklyn.

"Ned rang the doorbell and a husky middle-aged man in a bathrobe answered the door. He had a drink in his hand. His face was a fiery red that extended over his bald head.

"Ned introduced me to the director, whose name was George. We followed him through the hall to a spacious living room with several abstract paintings on the wall and a thick green carpet on the floor with some young men and women sprawled on it. The only furniture in the room was a long low sofa, a stereo set, and a coffee table.

"George introduced me to the young people. They muttered hello and then went back to their conversation. I didn't get any of their names, but I couldn't ask them to repeat them because they were all so caught up in their talk.

"The director asked us what we'd like to drink. I asked for wine. Ned wanted Scotch on the rocks and Theodore ordered a dry martini.

"When George came back with our drinks, he sat on the floor and a very fat girl with a beautiful face and long shining blond hair put her head on his lap and he played with it while he talked to Ned and Theodore.

"I felt ill at ease. No one seemed interested in talking to me. Pieces of conversation floated to me. They all seemed to be discussing a young male dancer who had decided he could fly and died doing a swan leap from his window. One girl was saying, 'He wasn't a great dancer, but he was the spirit of modern dance.' Everyone seemed to agree.

"A man said, 'I remember the day he came to tell me he'd decided to give up painting and become a dancer. I laughed at him and told him he was too old to start dancing. But he said he felt he had to dance. And two months later he had a part dancing in a show.'

"I kept wishing I had known the dancer. He sounded like a beautiful person. And, besides, then I would have been able to join in the conversation.

"George asked me if I'd like to see some of his movies. I said yes. I was very excited. When he announced he was going to show them, some of the people started complaining, 'Oh, don't put us through those again.'

"But he laughed and said, 'It's a command performance. We have a new audience here.'

"The fat girl with the lovely hair got up and started pulling down the shades while George got the films and the projector together.

"I had never seen movies like that before. The first movie opened with a naked woman being dragged by two naked men. The men wore sunglasses, caps, shoes, and socks.

"They tied the woman to a bed. Then they started hitting her with a rope. The films were silent, but I imagined I could hear the woman's screams.

"The two men didn't really seem interested in hurting the woman, though. They were sort of joking around. The shorter man, who had a flabby stomach, took off his hat and started beating the woman with it. Then he put his sunglasses on her and continued beating her with the rope.

"Finally the men untied the woman and handed her the rope and got down on their hands and knees so she could beat them.

"The second movie was the story of a man and woman on a ship who meet at the bar and go to his cabin to make love. It reminded me of other movies I'd seen except that it didn't fade out when the couple started undressing.

"The camera stayed on them until everything was over. I'd never seen two people making love before and found myself wondering if I could let someone make love to me in front of the camera.

"Back in Indiana, my boyfriend Al had made love to me a few times but it had hurt so much I couldn't enjoy it. But Al had told me I would get used to it and it wouldn't hurt any more and I'd really enjoy it as much as he did.

"The girl in the movie seemed to be delirious with happiness. But, of course, she could have been only acting.

"Ned and Theodore were in the third movie and I was shocked to see them making love to each other. I wondered if it was only for the film or if they were really in love with each other. They did seem very serious.

"When the films ended, George turned the lights back on and asked me how I'd liked the movies. I told him I thought they were very original and everyone laughed.

"George wanted to know if I'd like to act in one of his movies. I blushed, but I told him I would. He told me he was making a movie next week and would pay me twenty dollars a day for every day they shot. I told him I'd be there.

"Ned and Theodore asked me if I'd like to leave with them. I told George goodbye and promised to see him next Monday.

"Ned said he and Theodore were going home and they offered to drop me anyplace I wanted to go. I told them I didn't have any place to go, and they said I could stay with them in their apartment on Horatio Street in the Village. I was only too happy to accept.

"They had a nice, artistic apartment with a big living room, two bedrooms, a kitchen, and a bath. Theodore and Ned shared one bedroom and gave me the other.

" 'Please feel at home,' Theodore told me. I liked them both, and wasn't lying at all when I told them I did feel at home.

"Ned and Theodore took good care of me. Ned said I was their little sister and they treated me that way, cooking food for me, not allowing me to do any housework, asking me if I needed anything. It was such a change from home.

"They told me I could stay with them as long as I wanted to. They bought me wonderful, sophisticated clothes and seemed to enjoy dressing me up.

"Ned was very good at styling women's hair and he gave me a sexy French hair style that reminded me of Brigi Bardot except that me hair was light brown, not blond. Ned washed my hair with a cream rinse that made it lighter and more silky. I couldn't believe it was really me when I looked at myself in the mirror.

"When the day for filming arrived, I was terribly excited. I couldn't eat any of the breakfast Ned cooked for me. I dressed up in my most sophisticated new dress, a black sheath, and Ned insisted on combing my hair for me.

"The boys did everything they could to make me feel more relaxed.

" 'You look gorgeous,' Theodore told me. 'I'm sure George will make you the star of the movie.'

" 'He'll be a fool if he doesn't,' Ned said.

"George was impressed by my appearance. 'I hadn't realized how lovely you were,' he said, patting my cheeks with his soft, fat, sweaty hands. 'I have a nice part for you. But first let me get you all a drink.'

"His slippers flopped up and down as he walked toward the kitchen. The same crowd who had been talking of the dead dancer were once again spread out on the floor. But this time no one was talking. They were all drinking and staring into space as though they were each viewing their private vision.

"I sat on the sofa next to Ned. 'Drink your liquor first,' Ned whispered to me. 'It'll help you relax.'

"When George came with the drinks, I followed Ned's advice and finished mine in one long gulp that almost strangled me. I felt my head growing lighter right away.

" 'Let me get you another drink,' George said. I started to refuse, but Ned shook his head, so I accepted. The second drink made me feel very secure and relaxed. I smiled at Ned and he returned the smile.

"George stood in the middle of the room holding his glass. His face was red, his stomach hung heavily in front of him. 'First, let me explain the movie to you,' he told me. As you all know, I never use a script, so we'll all be improvising. The name of the movie, at least the working title, is '*The Sofa*,' and all of the action will take place on the sofa.

" 'What I had in mind was to show the sexual life of one sofa, all the various types of sex that take place in the lifetime of one sofa. So far, I've thought of a married couple who quarrel and make up having sex, a young virgin who has her first sex on a sofa, two men who have sex with each other, and the finale will be an orgy which will include the entire cast. Naturally, I'll be eager to hear all of your suggestions.'

"The fat girl with the lovely hair and face asked, 'Why is it always two men making love? Why not two women?'

" 'You're right,' George said making a note of it. 'We'll have two girls also.'

" 'What about a rape scene?' a plump young man with a red face and blond curly hair asked.

" 'Well, I was thinking of the virgin as a sort of subtle rape. You know, the girl goes so far and says stop, but the boy forces her the rest of the way. We'll see how it works out. I don't feel we should have two rapes. But if this scene doesn't end up with a slight rape, we'll have to include another rape scene. Any more suggestions?'

"There were none. 'Okay. The first scene I'd like to shoot is the virgin. I believe our new little actress would be very good in this role. Are you a virgin?' he asked, turning to me.

" 'No. I'm not a virgin,' I said. 'Not any more.'

"Everyone laughed.

"George patted my arm. 'That's good,' he said. 'I wouldn't want you to lose your virginity in front of the camera. Although that is an idea. We must try it one day. If we can ever find a virgin who's willing.

" 'Anyway, Fifi, how do you feel about playing this part?'

" 'I'd love to,' I said.

" 'Fine. Now let me see who shall play the man. He looked around the room slowly, examining all the males.

"I followed his eyes, hoping he'd choose Ned or Theodore because I didn't like the idea of making love to someone I really didn't know, not even if it was only acting. I saw him looking intently at the fat, curly-haired boy who'd suggested a rape scene. I hoped he didn't choose him. I didn't like him at all. I would rather have done the scene with anyone else in the room. But George did choose him. 'Tony, how'd you like to be the hero of this little scene?'

"Tony smiled and said, 'Suits me fine.'

" 'Okay. Let's get down to business then. As I see it, the two of you have just returned from a date. Fifi has asked you in for coffee. You've had the coffee and you're directing her to the sofa so you can start making out. We start shooting as you two sit down on the sofa.'

"He turned to me. 'Do you understand your role? You're in love with Tony, but you're a virgin and you don't want to let your virginity go, not too easily, anyway. Play hard to get. Try to get into the part. Once you're really in it, do anything you feel like doing. Just remember, the whole scene should last no more than thirty minutes and twenty should be spent having sex. So don't play too hard to get.'

"George and the photographer started setting up the cameras.

" 'Are we going to rehearse it?' I asked.

" 'We never rehearse,' George said. 'I like spontaneity. If it doesn't work out, we'll shoot it again. But the first time is usually the most real.

" 'Okay. It's up to you two. Tell me when you're ready.'

" 'Suppose we start on the sofa with me kissing her and my hands start roving and she pushes me away and go on from there?' Tony suggested.

" 'It sounds good to me,' I said. I felt frightened at the idea of someone

making love to me in front of the camera and all those people. I
wondered if it would hurt as much as it had when Al made love to me.
Once I started thinking of the pain I didn't think too much of the people
watching except for wondering what they'd think of me once they
realized I was almost a virgin.I wished I had let Al make love to me many
more times so I wouldn't be so nervous now. Well, it would have been
much worse if Al had never done anything.

"Tony kissed me on the cheek and said, 'Good luck, honey. I know
you'll do a fantastic job.'

"And Theodore said! 'Give it all you got, baby.'

"I felt better then. Tony started kissing me. His kiss was hard and
demanding. His tongue plunged almost down my throat and made me
feel like I was going to vomit.

" 'Well, I have to start somewhere,' I thought. 'I'm going to be a movie
star and nothing is going to stop me. That's why I came to New York.'

"I forced myself to respond to the kiss. Tony's hand slipped between
my legs and under my dress. Automatically, I reached for it, trying to
move it away. He kissed me more violently and touched my breast. I
reached for his hand again.

" 'Come on, baby,' Tony said seriously, 'don't be *that* hard to get.'

"I remembered that we were acting and let him reach under my dress
and slip under my panties. I touched his arm again, trying to pull it away,
but he kept on.

"I was surprised to realize his hand felt good on my body, warm and
soft. I opened my legs and relaxed.

"He slipped my panties off and dropped them onto the floor. This was
the way it had been with Al. He had made me feel so good before the
pain.

'You're doing fine,'Tony whispered in my ear.

"I relaxed a little more and he gently pushed me down and climbed on
top of me. I hardly noticed when he slipped out of his pants.

" 'Pull her dress up more,' George said, 'Give us a nice shot of her little
bottom.'

"Tony slid off me then, turned me on my stomach, raised my dress to
my waist and gently kissed my bottom. Then he rolled me onto my back,
kissed me down below, and lay down on me kissing my mouth.

"I felt his thing between my legs then, and the pain.

" 'You really are a virgin!' Tony said.

" 'You're hurting me!' I told him.

" 'Don't stop now,' George said. 'This is great.'

"The pain was getting worse. I felt like I'd have to scream. I bit my lips
and twisted underneath him.

"George held the camera over my face. 'Beautiful,' he said.

"When the scene ended, everyone congratulated me. Ned and Theodore were so proud. 'You did a beautiful job,' Theodore told me. 'I knew you could do it.'

" 'You're a great actress,' George said.

"Ned kissed me on the cheek and whispered, 'I hope it didn't hurt you too much. I suffered with you. But you looked so beautiful. I know you're going to be famous one day.'

"The fat girl with the lovely face and hair told me, 'You were absolutely great.'

"I felt like a famous actress. 'Thank you so very much,' I said. 'I'm glad you enjoyed it.'

"George sent out for lunch then and we all relaxed.

"Ned offered me a cigarette. I decided to smoke to look more sophisticated. He told me softly, 'You should have told me you were a virgin and I never would have let you go through that. Not that you didn't do a great job, but acting is one thing and sex is another.

"The first time you have sex it should be something pure, something beautiful. After that you can separate it, but the first time you deserve more.'

" 'Oh, it wasn't the first time,' I told him. 'My boyfriend Al made love to me a couple of times.'

"That seemed to satisfy Ned. 'I'm glad,' he said. 'You frightened me. If I thought we had ruined sex for you I'd never forgive myself.'

" 'I feel fine,' I told him. 'Nothing is ruined.'

" 'I'm so relieved,' Ned said.

"In the weeks after that, I played many roles in George:s films and soon I felt more relaxed in front of the camera than I did away from it.

"I became George's favorite actress because he said I had a fresh naive appearance of virginity and yet I'd agree to play the most daring scenes, scenes that the other girls would refuse to do.

'I got to be a sort of porno star,' Frances told me proudly.

Some runaways, like Frances, don't even realize when they are being exploited. She actually felt the film director was helping her achieve her ambition to become a movie star.

Quite a few young runaways have readily agreed to pose for pornographic pictures because the photographers promised to make them famous models. Recently there was a big scandal when it became known that a man had put ads in underground newspapers for young models. He paid good money and not only attracted young runaways, but even parents who brought their young children to pose in all sorts of obscene poses because the pay was so high.

It was even rumored that he took photos of fathers making love to their own daughters. This particular man then put ads in those same newspapers, selling the pictures he had taken, and made a great deal of money before he was arrested. Men like him are one of the dangers kids away from home face. Another recent news story reported a thirteen-year-old runaway who had been indoctrinated into commercialized sex in Norfolk, Virginia. The girl had come there after fleeing her home in Paterson, New Jersey, and had answered a newspaper ad run by a massage parlor.

She told the police she worked there for three weeks as a masseuse, and had "turned two tricks" with customers. She had received sixty dollars, of which the operator took half.

Part of her job was to massage the customer's entire body with her breasts, for which she received two and a half dollars an hour. She received five dollars an hour for direct sexual stimulation of a customer. Youth Bureau Investigator John Materson was quoted as saying that the girl was forced to "perform all kinds of sexual acts with the managers and owners of these places."

When I asked Frances if she'd missed her family, she said, "Sure, I missed them. But I was afraid to write home because I knew I could never live there again, and I thought they might have called the cops, and if they knew where I was they might come after me. And sure enough, that's what finally happened.

"At Christmas time, I did start feeling pretty homesick. I bought a beautiful Christmas card and put a check for ten dollars in it and sent it to my mother asking her to get a little gift for everyone. I didn't put a return address on it, but the postmark said New York.

"And one afternoon, a week after Christmas, I was at a cafe in the Village having supper with Ned and Theodore. It was one of the places where a lot of gay people and theater people go.

"We were laughing and talking when all of a sudden, I heard my father saying, 'Frances, what in the hell are you doing in here?' At first I thought I was just dreaming. My father would never come to a place like this. But of course he had come looking for me.

" 'Frances, how could you do this to your mother and me?' he asked. 'We gave you a good Catholic upbringing and to see you turn out like this?'

"Ned and Theodore were with me, but my father ignored them completely and addressed all his statements to me. He pulled out an advertisement from a sexy underground newspaper with my picture in it, an ad for one of the movies I was in, and told me how heartbroken he had been when he'd first seen it.

"I knew my family would never see any of those pictures so I'd never worried about them. They only appeared in underground newspapers, but of course my father had come to New York as soon as they got the Christmas card and had looked everywhere and asked everyone in the street for advice on how to find a girl who'd run away.

"He was really mad at me, and he kept telling me over and over how I'd hurt everyone by running away and how he can't even tell Mother what I was doing in New York because it would actually kill her to know. He told me it had cost him his life savings to come to New York looking for me. 'I had to fly because I couldn't afford to be away too long. I still may lose my job. You'll never understand how much your lack of consideration has hurt our family.'

"He grabbed my arm and told me to get my coat. 'We're getting out of here,' he said.

"I was only too happy to leave the cafe for everyone was staring at us and a lot of the people were my friends and it was really embarrassing.

" 'I don't want to leave, Daddy,' I said. 'I won't go,' I told him.

" 'You'll come on your own or I'll call the police,' he threatened.

" 'Please, Daddy, I don't want to go home.'

"He grabbed me, almost picked me out of my seat and forced me to leave with him.

"Ned and Theodore sat there, looking stunned. I ran and kissed them goodbye, thanked them for all they had done for me. I was crying when I left and I think they were, too.

"Daddy took me to his hotel where he called Mother and told her he'd found me and made me talk to her. Mother was as angry as Daddy was and kept complaining about how much I'd hurt her and ruined their lives. She never stopped to think how miserable they'd made mine.

"Well, the next morning we flew back home to Indiana. It was really hell. They expected me to return to that same life that I had hated so much. It had been terrible before, but it was even worse now that I'd been out on my own and done what I wanted to do.

"I might have been able to stay home until I finished high school if my parents had made some little effort to understand my feelings and what I wanted out of life. At that time I did still love them and I had missed them. But they never even said they'd missed me. They just complained about the worry I'd caused them, the heartache, the money Daddy's trip had cost.

" 'I didn't ask you to make the trip,' I told him. 'I'm sorry you did. I was happy there. I didn't want to come home.'

"My mother started crying then and telling me how heartless I was. Well, I felt the same about them."

This points out how important it is when a runaway returns home, whether by choice or "other means," that the family take stock of the situation and strive to improve their relationship, to start anew, to give the kid a say.

For some lucky prodigals, their running away is the shock that opens the way to communication, but for Frances, it only served as another closed door. "They still treated me like a little girl. I'd been a sex symbol in movies and they still wouldn't let me go out on dates. Can you imagine?

"The first chance I got I wrote a long letter to Ned and Theodore, giving them a girl friend's address and asking them to send me some money. At first I was afraid they wouldn't, thinking they might be afraid to get into trouble because Daddy had threatened to have everyone connected with the films thrown into jail. Of course, he didn't do anything about it because he didn't want anyone to know I'd made that kind of film.

"Well, they did come through with the money, and as soon as it arrived, I got a friend to drive me to a bus station in the next town in case my dad had asked the people at our bus station to keep a lookout, since he knew I wanted to run away again.

"When I got back to New York I wanted to start making movies again, but Ned and Theodore said it was too dangerous because that's the first place Daddy would look, and they were afraid he'd call the police.

"He didn't because he cares more about the family reputation than he does about me. In fact, he knew what I was doing, so he decided that he'd rather not have me come home.

He had told me if I ran away again or if I ever did anything like make that kind of movies again, he would disown me and I guess he did. But that doesn't bother me, because I'd rather he disowned me than came looking for me again.

"I stayed with Ned and Theodore for awhile, but we were all uptight, worried that Dad just might find us since he had found me in that neighborhood the first time. I was looking for a job, but Ned and Theodore kept telling me I couldn't make any more films because we could all get in serious trouble, and I was only fifteen with no work experience. So there was nothing I could do. Finally I ran into an actress who was working as a barmaid in the Village. We became good friends and when I told her my problem, she invited me to move in with her.

"Sharon was a very nice girl. She was twenty-one and had been in some porno films, done some modeling, and been in some off-off Broadway shows. But she usually made her living as a barmaid. Sharon was very attractive. Tall with a good figure and a pretty face. She had lots of boyfriends but wasn't serious about any of them.

"One night when I was getting dressed she came and put perfume all over my body. 'You have a beautiful body,' she told me.

"She started caressing my breasts and the first thing I knew we were making love. It shouldn't have shocked me since I knew that Ned and Theodore made love and I'd even made love to women in a few of the earlier movies, but I'd been acting then and hadn't really felt anything. really felt anything.

"I did feel something for Sharon. In fact, I actually fell in love with her. We both went out with men, but we both knew that no man could come between us.

"I thought I was the first woman Sharon had made it with, but later on I found out she'd had quite a few girl friends before me. I didn't really mind, though.

"At first, we tried to keep it a secret that we were making it with each other-you know, to pretend that we were just roommates-but recently we joined Gay Liberation and now we're proud of our relationship. It makes us sort of special.

"Most of our men friends are gay, too, now, so we don't have to worry about getting jealous of a man coming between us. I'm really happy now, happier than I've ever been in my life, except maybe for the time when I was making movies.

"I'm just waiting to be old enough so that I can make a comeback and then I'll have everything I've ever wanted."

So this is the saga of the runaway porno queen who hasn't yet made it to Hollywood, but has been through all the hustle and bustle of her flesh. It is a little too early to say that seventeen-year-old Frances lived happily ever after. It's hard to know what tragedy may find her, how her life as a runaway may affect her life as she grows older, whether or not her attitudes will change; but, of course, that's true for many others.

"I don't care," she says.

She knows the future will be different, that growing up will bring its own expansions of time. She thinks experience is its own reward. But life is an existential duel with chance, and Frances may continue to stand outside herself and observe both pain and pleasure. She could become one with her motto: "Once I started thinking of the pain I didn't think too much of the people watching, except for wondering what they'd think of me once they realized I was almost a virgin."

At that age, vulnerable, groping for meaning and understanding, even for acceptance, in a world that's fast and quick and brutal, all Frances thought of was appearances, even as she was learning to exploit her own naivete.

How could Frances remake herself as a high school girl when her body and her mind were totally different from her goalkeepers! She will have to free herself in her own way, to go beyond fearing her father and learn to relate to another human being wholesomely, outside of the pornographic mirrors.

And, think, what Frances survived, perhaps what she's still experiencing, is the story of countless other young girls trapped in their desire to make it in the city and by the fleshgods who have shamed them into believing that abandonment is a virtue and chastity the greatest sin of them all.

4
Karla And Her Friends

Wednesday morning at five o'clock
as the day begins,
silently closing her bedroom door,
leaving the note that
she hoped would say more,
she goes downstairs to the kitchen,
clutching her handkerchief,
quietly turning the back-door key¢
stepping outside, she is free.

When I first met Karla, her runaway days were already behind her. She was twenty-seven, had made peace with her family many years before, and had just recently decided that the suburban life her parents lived was nothing like the meaningless air-conditioned nightmare she had once imagined it to be.

In fact, after years of trying to make it on her own with waitress jobs and shabby lower East Side apartments with the toilets in the hall and bathtubs in the kitchens, she had realized that what she really wanted out of life was what her parents had, a nice conventional existence in a comfortable house with a stable, dependable husband and two kids. The dream reduced to its atomic simplicity.

And, at last, she was ready to talk about it, to understand the journey, even to rationalize the quest, perhaps merely to return in thought to the greatest adventures of her life, and words flowed in a torrent of pain and joy.

She was bold and up-front, her eyes openly meeting mine.

"I don't regret running away," she said. "I'm glad I left home when I did. At sixteen, I was being smothered by the sheltered life I was living. I was deathly bored of the same orderly routine, day after day.

"I felt I was living in a vacuum. Life was escaping me. It was something Out There where Beautiful People in black turtleneck sweaters and blue jeans had one great adventure after another as they followed the sun, crossed oceans, continents, and deserts; contemplated their navels until they reached Nirvana and then shared their insights with fascinating friends in coffeehouses and caves as they listened to cool jazz, avant-garde poetry, and deadly gossip.

"I'd sit alone in my room, where I was supposed to be doing my homework and I'd feel this terrible loneliness, this emptiness, this heavy sense of being outside of life, alone with my nose pressed against the glass, doomed to a lifetime of solitary confinement, a prisoner in the castle of my skin."

She'd watch her father going to his law office every day. Her mother taught high-school English and hurried home from classes each afternoon to take care of the house and cook supper. Sure, they really didn't seem to mind it that much, but Karla saw it as a living death, a weakening of the senses, and couldn't imagine a worse fate.

"But you loved them?" I was puzzled. Memory tinged with such ferocity.

"Sure. I always loved them."

But at sixteen she couldn't imagine a more meaningless existence. "And even though I know that's what I want for myself now, I would have been miserable if I had just stayed home, finished school, and married a nice boy without ever knowing any other life-style.

Now that she knows what it is like to be without the basic necessities and many of the luxuries of life, she feels she is better able to appreciate them. She would have continued to take them for granted, to resent the comfortable routine they afforded, and to long for other scenes and new adventures; to live in a dream instead of the present.

And look at her now with those bright eyes, that knowing smile. It took all those years of struggle to teach her that life is not always the big something around the next corner or over the next hill, a beautiful butterfly that constantly escapes your chase, that proverbial pot of gold at the end of the rainbow.

"I know now it's the rainbow and the rain and the butterfly. It's not the great prize that the future holds. It's right here, right now. I don't feel outside of life any more. I feel a part of it. That's why I can stop chasing my shadow and accept my parent's life-style, the life-style I used to find so repulsive."

At first, living with some impoverished kids in a lower East Side crash pad was an exciting, exotic, even glamorous way to live. She saw herself as one of the lucky ones.

She had actually rejected materialism.

"I was convinced I was a saint or something." She pinched herself. "And I really enjoyed my new life. I'd never had to worry about money or food or a place to live. I imagined myself an actress in a romantic movie as I walked the garbage-laden streets and climbed the filthy, dingy steps to our fifth-floor crash pad."

She would remind herself of how many people in the world go to bed hungry, never knowing if or when their next meal will come and how long the roof will remain over their heads, and felt a real bond with all the downtrodden of the earth. "With a smug smile I reminded myself that I had actually chosen to share their precarious situation."

But it never dawned on her in those early days that the great, admittedly eager sacrifice hadn't really profited anyone except Karla. She honestly felt that by rejecting middle-class materialistic values she was doing her part to make a better world, and never stopped to analyze just how her actions were to accomplish this great feat.

But as time went by, her new life-style appeared less and less glamorous and more and more of a hassle. After awhile you get tired of no heat in the winter, toilets that don't flush, junkie muggings in the hallway, stinking garbage piling up in front of your building, no hot water when you want to do the dishes or wash your hair. And it's hard not to become materialistic when you have to hustle for each meal and money to pay the rent or light bill.

After awhile you realize that poverty is easy to choose, but is a hell of a lot harder to get out of once you've chosen it.

Of course, she could always pick up a telephone and call Daddy, and he'd come get her and take her home to her nice warm room and three meals a day of Mama's good cooking. In that sense, she never knew what real poverty is, what it's like to not even have that one last resort, how frightening and depressing it must be to have absolutely nowhere to turn, no one to turn to.

But pride held her back. She wouldn't call. She knew her parents would be terribly worried, so she wrote them a note the very first week, saying she loved them and she was okay and not to worry. She continued to write at least once a month, but she was afraid to call, and never gave them her address. She would stay in control.

"I knew Mama would cry and me, too, and I'd break down and tell her everything, where I was and just how tough things were, and let her talk me into coming home."

But you always put off the return. After a few months, when home-sickness had really gotten to her, she was sorely tempted. But suddenly a whole new life opened up to her when Gale, a member of the crash pad, took her to a happening.

"We went to check out the scene and it turned out to be a sort of cooperative night club. Lots of people, most of them fairly young and everyone looking down and out, like this was their last chance at happiness.

"The man in charge called himself Jove. About fifty. Tall, big-boned, with long curly white hair and a flowing bushy beard.

"He spoke first. 'We are a group of people working together to become the most beautiful, loving, happy, artistic folks we can be. And since we were lucky enough to get this space we are going to make the most of it. That's why we've invited all of you here tonight. So, get up and express yourself any way you want. If you've always wanted to sing in public, dance, act, tell jokes, whatever, here's your chance.' "

"It turned out to be more of a group-therapy session than a performance. The crowd was really a collection of lost souls, desperately lonely people, much as my girl friend and I were, people reaching out for any kind of communication. After each of the pathetic attempts, the performers spoke of their feelings and there was a general discussion of the value in human terms.

"That first night, I believe, Jove spoke of he and his friends forming Mysta, a commune, and took down the names and addresses of people interested.

"The informal night club continued for a month or two. Gale and I went back once more to take some other friends who were interested in the commune. Although three weeks had passed since the first time, the scene was almost identical. The faces had changed, but the same sad, empty expressions were visible, owned by people who had given up all hope of ever finding an answer for any of their real questions or even the imitation of a cause worth living for."

About a month later, she read a flier about a poetry reading sponsored by Mysta. She and Gale decided to go to a storefront on the lower East Side, where members of the commune were then living and regularly giving poetry readings, community dinners, and the like to attract new recruits. Jove was an urban visionary. The spirits had told him he was to start Mysta. The women did all the housework and cooking, and took care of the young. The spirits had also told Jove the women were not to use any form of contraceptives. It boiled down that the women were to become breeders.

"I didn't even realize what this meant until I'd become a member. But at that point I was so sick of living in the crash pad, which was no more than an empty apartment someone had moved out of without the landlord's knowledge. A few runaways had just moved in and it was a real mess. Big holes in the floor. You had to watch where you walked or you might fall through. People came and went. We never had enough food. Nobody was working. Anything anyone had of value was stolen the first night they were there. Absolutely no privacy. There was no electricity after the first week I was there. At first it was romantic living by candlelight but after awhile it got to be a real bore. I love to read at night and reading by candlelight is a real bitch.

"So at that point Mysta looked very good to me. There were members of the group who had inherited money and Jove had a veteran's pension. They always had enough food to eat, soap, and warm water for baths even though you might have to share the bathroom with half a dozen other bodies.

"Jove's philosophy went on to say that the men were to be visionaries, the philosophers, the artists. The women were to live in one section with the children when they had enough space to do this, so that the men could devote their time to improving their minds and the world and not be bothered by children or daily tasks.

"At that point, however, they didn't have enough space to put this into practice, although the women did do most of the housework, but none of us were into women's liberation so we really didn't notice how unfair it was."

Another person who joined Mysta at that time was a tiny woman named Barbara. She was about five feet tall, weighed ninety-five pounds, had freckles on her nose, and shoulder-length hair with bangs. She never used make-up, and usually wore faded blue jeans. She had a little boy six years old whom she'd been raising on her own and she was happy to have the support that Mysta offered.

But Deidra, the runaway gypsy, she was the mother figure. They called her the Love Goddess. She was young, about eighteen, but had a way of assuming authority and responsibility. She saw that everything was in order, or her conception of order, which was frequently chaos.

She fell in love with Lee, a young writer who was looking for a guru and had joined the commune because Jove seemed to have a message. Lee was one of the lost souls from the co-op night club.

The basic rule was that everyone was to have sex with everyone else. Lee and Deidra wanted to make it only with each other. They were told, mostly by Jove, that was out. It was sort of a "Brave New World." Karla had been a virgin when she joined the commune. When she told them, they had agreed to go slow with her. They had let her alone, nobody pushing her to do anything, but she wasn't shocked by all the sex; there had always been a good deal of sex at the crash pad, too.

"Jove had had this vision and God told him to start a new religion and call it Mysta. Everybody was to love everybody else and live together like one big happy family. And God in His generosity told him we were to share everything and make ourselves happy and beautiful.

"If you took off your clothes to screw somebody, you might see your pants going out the door on one cat and some chick wearing your shirt. But all you had to do is look around and you could take anything that fit you. When we were at home we rarely ever wore clothes, because God had told us we shouldn't be too concerned with our clothes.

"The major sin in the religion was selfishness. When Deidra and Lee were still hung up on each other, Jove let it be known they'd have to get over their selfishness if they wanted to remain in the commune."

So they started making it with anyone who wanted to. However, Jove soon fell in love with two women. He immediately changed the rules. He only wanted to make it with a white waitress named Mildred and a black woman named Gloria, and he didn't want Mildred & Gloria making it with anyone but him. At that point it was decided that anyone in the group could have sex with everyone who wanted to, or he could limit himself. Complete freedom of desire and fulfillment.

Karla remembered the day she joined Mysta. As always, the front door was unlocked. The living room was dimly lit with a red bulb. Dinah Washington was singing "Love Walked Right In" over the hi-fi. Deidra, Lee, Barbara, and Netty, mother of two young kids at the commune, were sitting naked at the large round, old-fashioned table. "Join us," Deidra said. "We're finding out the future on the Ouija board. His name is Stu and he's a Persian poet.

"We used the Ouija board to find out exactly who should be a member of Mysta. You may notice that a lot of hanger-ons are gone. That's because Stu said they were out. We asked Stu about you and he said you're in."

Lee changed the subject. "Stu just told us there's a dark dagger hanging over the world and before the end of this century a great deal of fire will destroy everything except the beautiful people and we shall inherit the earth and the beauties thereof."

"Sit down," Netty said. "It looks like he's ready to speak again."

Karla pulle a chair up to the table and joined them.

"The Ouija board," said Karla, "was large, with symbols of dragons, devils, angels, frogs, and snakes. Letters in fancy Gothic characters and at the foot of the board a large YES on one side and a large NO on the other. In the center of the board was a glass ball. Everyone was touching it lightly with one finger. I put one finger there also and had never seen anything like this.

"Suddenly the ball began to spin. It seemed to hesitate for a second, then ran out from under our control. We had a hard time keeping our fingers on it. It rushed over to one side of the board, paused for a moment, then ran back into the middle, spun again, then stopped.

"I couldn't understand it at all. It really seemed to be going of its own will.

" 'What is your name?' Deidra asked the board. 'We have to make sure it's still Stu,' she explained. 'If we should contact another spirit, we might not be able to control him. There are wicked as well as friendly spirits, you know. Stu is very friendly. He's been with me for years.'

" 'What is your name?' she asked again. Soon it began moving. It seemed to know exactly where it was going. First directly to S where it paused a minute, then to the next letter T for another pause, and on to U where it stayed.

" 'It is Stu,' Netty said.

"There seemed to be a general release of emotion, as if everyone had been a little afraid they'd be confronted with a strange, harmful spirit.

" 'Stu,' Netty asked, looking anxious, 'when the world is destroyed, will my kids and me survive?'

"We put our fingers lightly on the ball. I tried to give it a little shove towards YES to make Netty happy, but the ball resisted. It seemed once more to have a mind of its own. Or, perhaps it was the force of the others pulling it. Or, maybe it really was Stu. Anyway, the ball began spinning, then it started running. It ran to F, and back to the center, then to YOUAREBEAUTIFUL, zigging toward the center between each letter.

" 'If I am beautiful,' Netty said, 'of course, that's true for all of us. I'm so glad Stu answered it that way so we don't have to ask about each of us individually.'

" 'Don't you realize,' Deidra interrupted, 'Stu was trying to tell you how wrong it was for you to be concerned with your own little self? Had you really been as beautiful as you should be, you never would have asked such a question. Don't you see how it was loaded with EGO?'

" 'I guess you're right,' Netty said. 'There are so many things I must work on.'

" 'Who wants to ask the next question?' Deidra looked around. All of a sudden I realized I had to get to the toilet right away if I didn't want to wet my pants.

"I hurried down the hall. The bathroom door was wide open and the room was overflowing with people. A huge black man was sitting on the commode with his pants down around his ankles. He was grunting and groaning as though he were giving birth to a mountain. An attractive young woman was brushing her long black hair in front of the mirror, naked as the day she was born. And Jove was making love to Mildred in the bathtub, which was full of water. It was the first time I've even seen Jove naked. He had a good, muscular shape except for a hanging belly.

"He and Mildred were splashing soapy water all over the floor.

"I poked my head inside the room, realized there was no room for anyone else, and started to back out.

" 'Want to use the bathroom?' Jove asks.

" 'I just wanted to pee,' I said.

" 'Do it in this glass,' the woman who had been brushing her hair said, handing me a plastic glass.

"I knew I had to do something right away so, feeling very self-conscious, I forced myself to use the glass and emptied the contents down the sink, carefully washing out the sink and the glass as rapidly as I could. Going to the toilet in front of an audience has always been very difficult for me and using a glass made me feel very sneaky, as though I should shut the door and run water so no one would know what I was doing. I was feeling a little embarrassed so I did my business as fast as I could and started out of the room.

"But Jove stopped me. 'Look in the medicine cabinet and see if there are any aspirins,' he said in his deep rich voice.

"The cabinet was crammed full of all sorts of tubes, bottles, and jars. Finally I came across a small bottle marked aspirins. I handed it to Jove but he asked me to pour him some water to take it with. The only glass in the room was the grimy-looking pale-blue plastic glass I'd just pissed in. I rinsed it out again, filled it with water, and handed it and two pills to Jove.

" 'Thanks a lot,' he said, and he gulped them down and handed me the plastic glass. I returned it to its place over the sink.

"The black man was still grunting over the toilet. Jove and Mildred went back to making love.

"When I returned to the living room, the group there had lost interest in the Ouija board. They were now deep in a discussion about how to kill the ego in order to become part of the Universal Self.

"Lee was saying, 'We should always behave in such a way that all of our actions could be repeated on a universal scale with the result of producing a more beautiful world. That is our goal on earth, to make ourselves beautiful so that we can spread beauty, create beautiful children, and beautify the world.'

" 'I don't know if I follow you,' Netty said. 'It seems to me that something could be beautiful when I do it and ugly when someone else does it.' She shook her head back and forth violently. 'Oh, that's not what I mean at all. What I mean is for an action to be beautiful the person doing it has to be beautiful, he has to think beautiful thoughts. If I have love in my heart, all my actions are beautiful. But, if I have hate I can do the same action and it would be ugly. Do you see what I mean?'

" 'I see you aren't following me,' Lee said. 'What I'm saying is beautiful actions make a person beautiful, and a person who has made himself beautiful through a long series of beautiful actions can perform only beautiful actions, whereas a person who has performed only ugly actions and failed to make himself beautiful can perform nothing but ugly actions.'

" 'I still can't follow you,' Netty said. 'It seems to me that nobody is all good or all beautiful, and nobody is all bad or all ugly, so all of us can do beautiful things as well as ugly things.'

" 'That's just the point Lee's trying to make,' Deidra said. 'It's up to each of us to make sure all of our actions are beautiful so that in the end we become completely beautiful and therefore incapable of any act which is not beautiful.'

" 'It sounds good,' Netty said, 'but not quite possible. I agree we should all try to be beautiful and do beautiful things but it seems to me it's impossible for anyone to become so completely beautiful that he never slips into an ugly action. Why, that would be perfection and once you've reach perfection you've no place to go.'

" 'What do you mean, you've no place to go?' Lee asked, becoming very excited. 'Perfection is just the starting point. Once we reach perfection we can really begin to live as beautiful people. We can relax and follow our inclinations, knowing that they will always lead us in the right direction. Only then can be begin to raise beautiful children and to beautify the world. So long as we ourselves have defects it's our obligation to work on improving ourselves and we have no time to beautify the world.'

" 'But we're part of the world!' Netty said, getting equally excited. 'And it seems to me when we make ourselves more beautiful we automatically make the world a little more beautiful.'

"Lee's eyes were twinkling. He dismissed the entire conversation wotj 'You have a way of twisting everything around.'

"He directed himself to Deidra. 'Remember when Jove was telling us how he felt about art? No matter what point he made, Netty interpreted it in her own way.'

"Life in the commune was a series of intellectual discussions.

"He turned to me. 'Jove feels that all art is important¢music, painting, poetry, dance, every art form¢because it helps make the artist more beautiful. He feels that the creative act is the most important thing and the art object is merely a by-product. The highest art is life, and once a person has made himself beautiful through creating art objects, what we usually think of as art ceases to have any importance whatsoever. A beautiful person has no need for art because his entire life has become

ART. So Jove has the highest respect for an artist, but he places no value at all on art objects per se.'

" 'I think Jove is right,' Netty said. 'Art can make the artist more beautiful and a beautiful life is the highest possible art. But it seems to me a beautiful work of art has a value of its own, has a life of its own, like a child. I can't imagine a world without painting, music, and poetry. When I hear a song that moves my soul or read a novel that says, 'You're alive, dig your life, make the most of every second,' or look at a painting that tells me, 'See how lovely the world is' or 'See how beautiful we are,' I do feel more alive, more beautiful. I can't believe art is just to make the artist beautiful. It's to make all of us beautiful.

" 'So the work of art is just as important as the act of creating it. I wouldn't want to live in a world without music and paintings and sculpture and books. Not even if every single person in that world were beautiful.'

"Lee gave a sigh of disgust. 'That just shows how far you are from understanding Jove's ideas! In a world where everyone is beautiful the air is full of music, not what we think of as music now but something a thousand times more moving because it's real. All the works of art we have today are imitations of life as it should be, life as it would be if everyone were beautiful. Art is useful today because it helps us to get a glimpse of eternity, it teaches us to see and feel beauty.'

" 'Robert Browning once said, "A painting makes us see a thing we've passed a hundred times and never seen before." But, once we all become beautiful and we live our lives as artists, we won't have to look at a picture of a tree in order to get a glimpse of all the mysteries a tree can hold. We'll see every tree we pass. We won't need to look at an artist's conception of a sky to know all the wonders the sky holds. Every time we look up we'll feel the magic that comes from recognizing the beauty in a sunset, a stormy sky, or a blue sunny day sky.'

" 'Once we're beautiful and really alive, we'll hear the music of the universe, see the dance of the trees, the birds, two flies making love, recognizing all the beauty in every object. We won't need an artist to interpret them for us any more than we'd need a language interpreter if we spoke every language. Our lives will be so full of the real beauties of life, we won't have any space for imitations no matter how realistic or inspired.'

" 'You make it sound so wonderful,' Netty told him, looking dreamy-eyed, 'but I still can't imagine living without ever seeing a painting or reading a poem.'

" 'I give up on you,' Lee said. But he continued his harangue. 'To become beautiful we have to develop the eyes of a painter, the hands of a sculptor, the ears of a musician, the words of a poet, the thoughts of a philosopher, the imagination of a writer, the free movements of a dancer.'

"A handsome young teen-age boy came into the room at that moment.

" 'Oh, wow! Netty said. 'I want to be the first to make it with you,' she told the young man.

"He blushed.

"Lee went on talking. 'That's what art can teach us¢to recognize the significance of the smallest object, to realize that now is eternity, to join our personal rhythms to that of the spheres, to live life actively instead of being a mere object acted upon. And once art has served its purpose of making us complete human beings, we must drop it as a snake sheds its old skin when it has grown a new one. That's what we need to learn, how to let go.'

"Such philosophical conversations were very frequent in Mysta. They became almost a way of life.

"I soon became very close to everyone in the group. But Netty became my best friend. It was hard to have deep personal conversations among so many people. I remember the first one I ever had with Netty. We had been sitting with the group during that long philosophical rap session. After several hours, Netty said, 'Let's find a spot where we can rap.' I followed her out of the living room and down the hall toward the toilet.

"She opened the first door we came to and we stepped inside. She flipped on the light and there on the bed was the black man who had been on the commode and the naked woman who had been combing her long black hair when I went to the bathroom.

" 'Have fun!' Netty told them and switched off the light again. The man and woman were too busy to answer.

"Netty put her finger to her mouth to warn me not to make any noise. Then she opened the door across the hall. There was a dim blue light in the room and a mattress spread out on the floor. A little naked boy about three years old with long brown hair was sound asleep, face down, on top of a huge plastic doll as long and as naked as he was.

"Netty shook her head sadly, backed out of the room, and closed the door. 'Poor little Mathew,' she said. 'Everybody else has someone to love. He's so lonely he has to make love to the doll. I tried to get my two kids to sleep with him so he wouldn't be so lonesome. But they're spoiled and insist on sleeping with me.'

"We entered the next bedroom. It was empty. Netty sat on the bed and started talking. 'The kids here say I raise my babies badly. They say I'm making them too dependent on me. Lee gives me long lectures about how I'll never be able to dig my kids as equals unless I cut the apron strings. I am sort of tied to them. You see, every time I want to go someplace they start crying so I stay home.'

" 'But Mathew's mother has freed herself. She can go and come as she pleases and Mathew doesn't even notice. He considers all of us his parents. Jove says that's the way it should be. But I guess I am sort of jealous. I want to keep being the most important person in my kids' lives. Maybe it's unfair, but they're all I have and I need them.'

"She wrinkled her nose and asked me for a cigarette.

" 'That's not true either,' she continued. 'I have a home here, lots of people I love and who love me. I really dig it and I think it's great for the kids. They've been through some real hard times.'

"She took a long drag from her cigarette and blew out the smoke immediately.

" 'I really loved their father,' Netty said. 'Paul was such a wonderful guy and I loved him so much. I met him when I was sixteen, back in Chicago. Of course my family almost freaked out at the idea of me being involved with a black guy. They made it so hard for us to see each other that we decided to run away together. That's how I came to New York.'

" 'Things were beautiful at first. Paul found some odd jobs and we were able to rent a little place on the lower East Side. But he had a terrible temper. He used to lose all control of himself. Just go crazy. He tried to kill me several times.'

" 'And you stayed with him?' I asked, surprised.

" 'I loved him. I remember the worst time. It was when I was pregnant with Lonnie and Mavis was only eight months old. Paul couldn't find a job. He had gone for an interview, and the boss very openly told him that although he himself was not prejudiced, the owner of the company did not want a black on the payroll. Paul got so upset he slugged the guy. Lucky enough, the guy didn't call the cops. He just kicked Paul out.'

" 'Paul took the last of our money, the money we had borrowed for carfare and milk for Mavis and he bought a bottle of whiskey. As soon as he walked inside the house, I asked him for Mavis's milk and he started shouting at me. 'Where do you expect me to get money for milk? I'm an unemployed nigger.'

" 'But you had some money this morning

" 'Then he took out the whiskey and started drinking it. I started screaming then, cursing him out for wasting money on alcohol when his baby daughter was starving. He really freaked out then. Why didn't I go out and money to feed her? I was white and it wouldn't be so hard for me. Finally he said, 'If you'd sell your pussy instead of giving it away, we could all eat.'

" 'I was so upset. I called him a nigger. I'd never said it before and never said it again. But he had hurt me so much I wanted to hurt him the same way.'

" 'He stood there staring at me for a second. 'So it finally comes out, huh? That's what you think of me. You white bastards are all alike. All racists. So why are you worrying about whether or not Mavis eats? She's a nigger just like her father.'

" 'We kept throwing insults back and forth, hurting each other as only lovers can, and suddenly he picked up a regular kitchen knife and plunged it into my stomach, saying, 'You hate niggers, do you? Well, I'll do you a big favor and kill that little black bastard you got in your belly.'

" 'I ran out into the hall and the neighbors helped me, all the time making digs about how a white woman should never marry a black because he takes all his hate out on her. Shit! If that's true, nobody should ever get married because most married people take their hate and frustrations out on each other.'

" 'I wasn't seriously hurt. It was a plain table knife and it barely pierced my flesh. But it had scared me and all the neighbors made such a fuss about it. Paul never really forgave me for bringing our white neighbors in on our affairs. But I was so scared I didn't know what else to do. If I hadn't gotten out when I did, I'm sure he would have killed me. He was so mad.'

" 'Life gets real messed up sometimes,' I said.

"Netty agreed. "It's sheer hell when two people really love each other like Paul and I do, I mean did, and things fall apart. When scenes like that keep happening, you can't imagine living apart but you're afraid to stay together. I mean, I was actually physically afraid of Paul. Afraid he'd really murder me or one of the kids.'

" 'Each time something awful like that happened I'd leave him. Go as far away and screw as many cats as I could, trying to force myself to get him out of my heart. But I never could. And every time I went back to him, there he was living with another girl. Even though he used to keep writing me and calling me and begging me to come back, saying he'd kill himself if I didn't. He'd introduce me to the girl as his wife and she'd be as embarrassed as hell and get out right away.'

" 'Things would be beautiful with us for awhile. Paul wouldn't touch a drink of liquor. He'd accept any kind of job he could get and our joy at being together again would help calm us both down. Then something would go wrong, and we'd be at each other's throats again, saying awful things that could never be unsaid and driving the poor babies crazy with our screaming and carrying-on. They'd start crying hysterically and Paul would threaten to kill all four of us, and I'd grab the kids and leave again. It was heaven when things went smoothly and hell when they didn't.'

"Netty chain-smoked as she talked. 'Jove says no matter how strong a love may be, once it's been patched up so many times it just can't hold up indefinitely, and the sooner the people involved call it quits the easier. I guess he's right. But sometimes when I remember the happy times I'm tempted to go back to Paul. I have to force myself to think of how awful the bad times were.'

"Netty was only eighteen and looked much younger. I couldn't believe that she'd actually gone through all the torments she described, but her intensity convinced me she had.

"'You know,' she said, "it's funny. People have a way of forgetting all the horrible things that happen to them and remembering the beautiful ones. I guess that's the only way we can keep on living without going mad or committing suicide. No matter how awful the past was, our memory has a way of making it so beautiful we find ourselves wanting to go back to it.'

"It sounded strange when Netty said that, but since then I've come to believe it's true.

"Netty had been through some terrible experiences. She told me about how her father found her and came to the house where she was living with Paul and the two babies and tried to force her to come home with him. When she refused, he left in an angry huff and returned with two policemen who took her to Bellevue for psychiatric examinations.

"'I had just turned eighteen, so I was old enough to be on my own, but they kept me in the hospital for two weeks for surveillance. A nuthouse is enough to drive anyone mad. I was sure I'd never get out of there. But after two weeks they released me. Shortly after that I joined Mysta. I wanted Paul to join. I thought we could all be happy here, but he refused. So I decided to try it on my own with just the kids. I miss him so terribly at times. It's almost a physical ache, but I'm convinced what I did was best.'

"I told her it sounded to me like she'd made the right choice.

"I was glad I had joined Mysta. It was so wonderful being part of a family and having some of the basic necessities of life, not having to worry about where the next meal was coming from, and having more experienced people around.

"But a few weeks after I joined, the police raided Mysta. Everyone at the commune was arrested for possession of drugs and for impairing the morals of minors.

"It seemed like the raid was planned. The police found a young man carrying marijuana in the hall of our building. They dragged him into our apartment, which was easy since we never locked the door. Of course, they found all of us naked as usual. The kids were naked, too, but they were asleep.

"The kids were put into foster homes, while the rest of us were thrown in jail. Jove had a record of a previous arrest. Six months earlier he had gone into a police station and offered all the policemen joints. Naturally, he'd been arrested for that.

"Since no one besides Jove had ever been arrested before, the rest of us were released after a few days. The group sort of scattered after that, although it got back together with different combinations of people from time to time.

Even though Karla had never been arrested before, the whole process was rather nerve-racking for her. She had shown the police her false identification papers, and since she was sixteen at the time but looked older, they had had no reason to suspect that she was a runaway.

Karla and Netty got an apartment together. After quite a struggle, Netty managed to get her two children back from the foster home where they'd stayed while she was in jail.

Times were changing rapidly. Karla landed a job as a waitress in a coffee shop. It didn't pay much, but she got her meals and it did pay her share of the apartment's expenses.

Only then did she make her first phone call to her parents. They begged her to return home. She agreed to come and spend the weekend, and to enroll in some evening courses in the Village toward a high-school diploma if they'd allow her to continue living on the lower East Side.

"I guess they decided that since I'd been able to make it on my own that long they'd let me continue; and, anyway, they knew I'd probably run away again if they forced me to stay home, so they agreed to leave me on my own.

"We all had a good cry. They did try to persuade me I should stay home until I finished high school; but although I must admit I was tempted, I knew I had to prove to myself and to them that I could make it on my own."

She did agree to permit her father to install a phone and to let him pay the phone bill, so they could be in close touch and she could call them in case of emergency.

"And I accepted the hundred dollars he gave me as a belated birthday present since I hadn't been home to celebrate it with them. But I refused to let him talk me into giving up my job and going to school full time while he supported me."

She went to school at night for one year. One of her teachers suggested she take some tests to get into an experimental program in one of the universities in the city, where they were taking kids without high school degrees who could pass the entrance exams. She got in and supported herself the first year by waitressing! Then with scholarships and loans (which she has since paid off by herself), and finally got her B.A. in Liberal Arts.

But as far as jobs were concerned, the diploma didn't help her much. She still couldn't get a decent job. She had no special talents, no experience, and her college work had been so general. Of course, she had long since given up her desire for a glorified life of poverty, but she was determined to raise her standard of living on her own.

After several years of trying to find the right job, one that she enjoyed and at the same time paid enough to allow her to return to a more comfortable life-style, she let her father talk her into accepting a gift of six months enrollment at a baking school in Switzerland. She enjoyed the trip and the school and was convinced she'd like work as a baker, but once she got back to New York and got a baking job, she soon discovered it wasn't exactly what she had been looking for.

"I'm really glad I studied baking. I don't feel it was a waste of time because some of my greatest joy has come from baking my own cakes and pies and breads, but I made the painful discovery that anything you do for a living becomes work after awhile and loses much of its pleasure-giving qualities."

So what was the missing ingredient?

"What I really need now is a good man who'll give my life some focus. I know that sounds unenlightened in today's women's-lib world, but I belonged to a consciousness-raising group for six months so my consciousness is raised. I did my man-hating time, so now I'm ready to settle down and take care of a man who will support me and give me some children and share my pains and pleasures. I agree with the women's movement that no woman should be forced to be a housewife. Every woman should be allowed to decide exactly what she wants to do with her life, and after much thought I've made my decision. So while I wait for Mr. Right to come along, I'm trying to get myself together.

"As you can see," (we were in her lower East Side apartment, a major improvement, she assured me, over her earlier ones as this one had a private bathroom, wall-to-wall carpets, and comfortable, if inexpensive, furniture) "I still haven't been able to support myself in the style to which I wish to become accustomed once more, but I haven't given up."

The Karlas never give up.

Her case was unique in my experience with runaways. She was the only one I spoke with who so enthusiastically and completely accepted her parents' life-style, after being exposed to one that was quite different and much more difficult for her to cope with. Many other runaways come from backgrounds similar to Karla's, and most of them reestablish some kind of relationship with their parents, but Karla had come to the conclusion that their way of life was exactly what she'd been looking for, that she only had to leave it to appreciate it.

The vast majority of runaways become so caught up in alternate life-styles that they find it impossible to return to the mainstream of Establishment living. They may "infiltrate" the Establishment part time in order to earn a living, but they generally identify more with runaways, dropouts, throwaways, and other freaks that make up the sometimes, not so youthful, alternate culture. They become strange inhabitants of distant planets afloat within the city walls from which the world is seen up and down and sideways.

The Karlas, the Netties, the Barbaras, they keep talking. Though they may wish to separate themselves from the past, memory remains a relentless link and creates a civilization of feeling. Life goes on. You can run, but you can't hide. Especially not from yourself.

5
Cindy

Early one morning, four years ago, I received a phone call from my girl friend Mavis.

A call from Mavis has always meant only one thing¢a desperate cry for help.

"Cindy ran away," she told me. She was crying so hysterically that she had great difficulty talking. "She's only fourteen. She's been gone two days now. She's never done this before. I'm so worried.

"Anything could happen to her out there. She had been threatening to run away if I didn't leave Bob, but I didn't think she'd really do it. It's not like her. Will you help me find her? I'll kill myself if anything happens to her."

Cindy was a beautiful child. Her father was black and Mavis was white. Cindy had lovely golden skin and a long, thick Afro. I'd known her since she was ten. Now she was tall and thin, with a round baby face, huge brown eyes with thick black lashes, a turned-up nose, heart-warming smile, and a way of floating rather than walking.

She was always a creative child, writing poetry, keeping a literary diary, doing watercolors, and studying dance. She always had a pleasant, warm smile for everyone, a friendly word, and never complained about the unlikely situations foisted upon her by her mother's disorderly life. But she loved Mavis too much to stand quietly and watch her throw her life out the window.

I remembered one family scene I had witnessed that might explain why Cindy had run away. Some kids are forced to run away to find a home, or at least an imitation of home that never be worse than the excuse for a home they leave.

Cindy's mother Mavis had been living with her boyfriend Bob for three years at that time, and breaking up from the time they first got together. Bob was not exactly an alcoholic, but he liked his liquor and couldn't handle it. It fired up his already stormy temper, and he'd end up taking out his frustrations with his feet or fist beating at Mavis's head. As a result, both Mavis and Cindy were terrified of him. Cindy because of concern for her mother; and Mavis, because of her awareness that Bob could very well kill her if he wished, and that you just never could tell with him.

As if the beatings weren't frightening enough, Bob had recently bought himself a switchblade and liked to play with it whenever he and Mavis had a "serious discussion" of their relationship.

Mavis and Cindy came to my apartment many times to hide from Bob after he'd threatened Mavis or beat her up. Mavis would tell me how horrible he was, how afraid she was that he'd kill her, and how she had to hide from him, and if he should call or come by the apartment, I was to tell him I hadn't seen her. Then after a few tearful days of black coffee and endless cigarettes, Mavis would decide to call Bob, "just to see if he's feeding the dogs," or for whatever excuse she could come up with. She'd keep calling the house, and if there was no answer, she'd start worrying about where he was, whether he was with another woman, etc., etc. And after more tears, coffee, and cigarettes, when she finally reached him, she would beg him not to be angry and make an appointment to meet him somewhere on neutral grounds, "to discuss their problems," and inevitably she'd drag Cindy back to the unbearable home scene.

As the Bible says, the sins of the parents are visited upon their children, and the poor, sweet, fourteen-year-old Cindy was going through hell while Mavis tried to free herself from the terrors her own parents had piled on her. They had separated right after she was born, and she was shifted back and forth between them. She never had a chance to really feel herself a part of either "family," was always in-between, stranded on a raft of emotions and the desire to belong more solidly.

All her life she had wanted a family so badly. She was willing to put up with anything, even an unreasonable facsimile. She longed to relate deeply, to care for someone and in turn be loved for what she was, without any sense of pretense or obligation. But look what had happened. She and Cindy's father had repeated the pattern and broken up shortly after Cindy was born. He hadn't even bothered to marry her.

What a downer. So she embarked on a series of desperate attempts to find a man who would head her family, but catastrophe inevitably ended each of her efforts.

Intellectually, Mavis had come to realize that it was impossible to have any kind of home life with Bob, but her desire for roots was so strong that she was willing to sacrifice the warm relationship she had with her daughter Cindy for a chance to form "a real family" with Bob, a hopeless cause.

Cindy loved her mother as much as any child ever loved a parent, but at fourteen she was old enough to realize that Bob was completely destroying Mavis. And after becoming best friends with Anita, a young married Puerto Rican woman with a new baby, Cindy gave her mother her ultimatum: Either she left Bob for good or Cindy would run away.

Bob was acutely conscious of his blackness, Mavis's whiteness, and Cindy's blackness as a result of having a black father, and he had forbidden Cindy to visit her Puerto Rican friend with her Chinese-American husband on the grounds that they would turn Cindy against her own blackness. But Mavis knew that Cindy's friend Anita and her husband were kind, considerate, "together" people who truly cared about Cindy and she was happy that Cindy had had the good fortune to meet them.

On the basis of that friendship and pressed by Cindy's ultimatum, Mavis got up the courage to leave Bob once more. She agreed to let Cindy spend a few weeks with Anita while she "got herself together." She called me up and asked if she could spend some time with me while she looked for a new apartment in another section of New York, where Bob wouldn't be able to find her and kill her.

As always, I agreed.

Mavis spent two endless tear-splashed days before she asked me to go out with her to cash a check so that I could protect her should she run into Bob. We did run into Bob, of course, and he almost attacked her on the street.

After many threats and harsh words, the two of them ended up spending the night at my apartment, because Bob refused to leave without her, and Mavis was afraid to be alone with him at her own place. All evening they argued. Mavis cried and Bob kept switching his blade in and out as he glared at her with hate in his eyes.

The next morning Mavis asked me if Bob could spend a few days at my place while she and Cindy returned to her apartment to "get themselves together." With great misgivings, I agreed to the arrangement, anything to give Mavis and Cindy a chance at happiness or freedom from fear, but I refused to give Bob the key to my apartment, wary of what he might do with it in the future during one of his mad rages.

That was probably a serious mistake. I had assumed Randy, the young former runaway who'd been staying at my place, would be home each evening to let Bob in since Randy rarely went out at night, but as luck would have it, Randy chose Bob's first two nights to go out (as I did). And Bob, on his first night at my place, ended up waiting in the cold, damp hallway until Randy finally arrived to let him in. He sulked but remained silent. The second night, when the same thing happened, he waited awhile, then went into a wild rage that all of us suffered the brunt of.

Mavis had called me on Bob's second afternoon at my place to see how things were going, saying she couldn't come to visit me as she definitely didn't want to see Bob. She asked me to stop by her place that evening.

It was raining that night, but I was insensitive to any warning of disaster as I dressed Raphael in his rain cap and jacket and braved the storm to visit Mavis. We shared a small supper with her. When Raphael fell asleep at the TV, Mavis suggested we spend the night. I was quick to agree since it was raining even harder than when we left home.

She and I were having a cup of coffee when we heard the loud pounding on the door.

"Oh, my God," she gasped. "He's back."

"Don't let him in," I suggested. "He won't know there's anyone home."

"Raphael might wake up from the knocking and Bob would hear him and break down the door and kill all of us for sure. I'd better let him in."

Bob stormed in, cursing her and spitting out the story of how he'd been locked out of my place two nights in a row, and in what a terrible way Mavis had treated him "passing me on from place to place as if I was just an old suitcase. That's the lowest a man can get. The worst thing a woman can ever do to a man."

He was really upset. I could sense the coming of a real explosion. Mavis begged him to return with me, telling him I had the key and we'd have no more problems. "Give me the chance to be left alone with Cindy so we can calm down and get our heads and our home together."

Bob refused. "I'm not going anywhere until I'm ready to. I'm home, woman. Didn't you hear me? I'm a Man. A man can put up with just so much and then he has to put his foot down if he wants to remain a man. And by God, I'm not giving up my manhood for any woman."

"We can't stay here together," Mavis said. "We're at each other's throats. I guess I'll have to go home with Maryanne. I did so want a chance to relax and feel free in my own home."

She started crying.

"You're not going anywhere, woman," Bob roared. "You're going to climb into that bed and go to sleep."

"I can't stay here with you," Mavis sobbed. "And Cindy will be home in a few minutes. I don't want her to see me like this."

She blew her nose and wiped her red eyes.

"You get in that bed right now, woman," Bob shouted, "and get to sleep. That's an order. When Cindy comes home, she'll find you sleeping."

"I couldn't sleep."

"I order you to."

"Couldn't Cindy spend the night with her friend?" Mavis begged. "At least, give me that much. I don't want her seeing me like this. She'll know something is wrong."

"Cindy's staying right here," Bob shouted. "This is her home, and by God, there's no reason she can't stay in her own home!"

"You call THIS a home?" Mavis cried, her whole body shaking with sobs.

"Cindy's staying here," Bob hissed. "Didn't you hear me, woman? The three of us are sleeping here tonight. What's she doing out so late, anyway?" he asked.

"She went to a movie with Anita. She was supposed to be home at nine."

"Well, it's almost ten, woman!" (I had never heard anyone use the word "woman" with such scorn and hatred!) "When are you going to get yourself and your business together? Do I have to beat some sense into your head? Do I? Do I?"

He raised his arm threateningly. She quivered with fear "No, Bob!" She shouted. "Don't, Bob! Please don't!"

He lay into her. It was the first time I'd seen him hit her, although I'd heard him threaten it often enough, and she'd told me of the many times he had hit her.

He knocked her down on the floor. Her head hit the side of the refrigerator and she moaned. But Bob didn't stop. He kept hitting her, kicking at her body with both his sharp-toed shoes.

I was horrified. I felt absolutely helpless. I wanted to pull him off her but knew that in his insane anger he was wild enough to kill both of us and Raphael and Cindy, too, if he wanted to.

I whispered to Mavis I was going to call the police but she whitened, gasped, and said, "Don't, for God's sake."

I really didn't know what to do.

Deliberately, I decided to play it cool, to show no emotion, no censorship, and hoped he'd agree to let me spend the night; or better still, let Mavis go home with me, for I felt certain he'd try to kill her and maybe Cindy if I left them alone.

Anita brought Cindy home a little later. Bob had stopped beating Mavis, who was still sobbing hysterically but nervously trying to look okay. Bob was playing it cool, lying quietly on the bed pretending to sleep.

I whispered to Anita not to leave, and tried to talk Mavis into making a dash for the door with the rest of us.

"I can't go," she said. "Bob would kill me if I tried. You heard him and saw what he can do."

"You're safe with all of us," I assured her.

But she was panic-stricken.

Anita tried to talk Cindy into running out the door, but Mavis ordered her into bed. The child looked completely bewildered. Something terrible was happening and she couldn't figure out what it was. She looked from face to face, silently asking for help.

"You heard me," Mavis told her, "Get into bed."

Defeated, still not knowing what dark cloud hung over her, Cindy climbed into the loft bed and burst out crying.

Anita and I left. I hurriedly told her what had appened earlier.

"Let's call the police," she said.

"Mavis told me not to call them," I said. "I wanted to, but she got very upset when I mentioned it so I'm afraid to."

Anita invited Raphael and me to come inside for a cup of tea, and to discuss the situation and decide what course to take. As we drank, I told her and her husband Mike about Bob and Mavis's fight.

"Do you think Cindy is safe there?" Anita asked.

"I don't know," I said. "I'm worried about both of them. Bob was really acting crazy."

"Let's go get her," Mike suggested, turning to Anita.

I stayed with the children while they went to rescue Cindy. In about ten minutes they were back, with Cindy and a suitcase containing her clothes.

Her eyes were red, her face streaked with tears, and her whole body tense.

Anita and Mike told me they had gone to the door and shouted for Cindy. When she answered, they pulled her outside and told her to come with them.

Cindy seemed relieved to be out of that apartment. But she was very worried about her mother. "I'm afraid Bob will kill her," she said. "I've heard him tell her he would so many times. I don't know why she won't leave him. He's no good for her. He's ruining her life."

"That's her choice," Anita told Cindy. "She could leave him if she wanted to. You heard us asking her to leave. What pisses me off is the fact that she allows him to put you through this."

Cindy locked herself in the bathroom and cried for about twenty minutes, then went into the bedroom, lay on the bed and continued sobbing. After about an hour Cindy told us she couldn't sleep and wanted to go home because she was worried about her mother. But while we were discussing whether or not this was wise, Cindy finally cried herself to sleep.

Bob and Mavis continued to separate and get back together. With unbelievable patience, Cindy begged her mother to stop acting like a child, to get out of that bad scene, to start building a decent life for them both. But the tragedy of Mavis's life blinded her to the tragedy she was inflicting on her daughter. If only Mavis had had the presence of mind to pick up her little girl and run away with her, things might have been different and Cindy wouldn't have had to run away on her own.

But Mavis didn't, and finally Cindy's patience ran out and she was forced to leave on her own, to become another young fugitive. Was she to blame? Who is to blame in this vicious cycle? Bob didn't ask to be born a poor black in a slum whose only out is alcohol. Mavis didn't ask to be born to parents who never made her feel wanted or gave her any kind of home.

The real problem is not who is to blame, but who will help. How can we stop this stupid, wasteful cycle? In most situations, there's still time to save young lives from going down the slimy drain and to repair those of their elders. Often, running away is a plaintive, desperate cry for help. If only parents and our society would see it as such, perhaps some of these children would be saved from the needless suffering that is the lot of the runaways as well as of those who stay at "home."

Every time I ran into Mavis she was depressed. She had received one letter from Cindy, postmarked San Francisco and telling her she missed her; that she hadn't wanted to go so far, but Bob wouldn't allow her to spend time with her friend Anita, and she couldn't stand the violence between Bob and her mother. Cindy had even called her mother a few times to make sure she was all right but wouldn't give her address, fearful that her mother would try to make her come home.

Cindy was gone for three and a half years before she returned home, thin and haggard from a drug problem and six months pregnant. She had a sad story to tell, but spoke easily of her life as a runaway:

"At first, I just went to St. Mark's Place a few blocks from home. I met some kids in the street. Told them I was looking for a ride out of New York.

"They helped me find one, taking me through the health-food stores, head shops, and bookstores digging on bulletin boards announcing rides. I found one to S.F. All I had to do was pay my share of the gas. Which was a gas.

"We ended up with six people in the car. Sure, it was crowded, but the kids were nice. I met a young Puerto Rican guy named Indio who promised to arrange a place for me to stay in Frisco.

"Indio was a nice guy, and he did take me to his friends, where we stayed together. The only problem was that they were all on drugs.

"I was so shocked the first time I saw Indio shooting up. He and his friends kept offering me smack, that's heroin. But I'm afraid of needles so I held out for several months.

"But after awhile they convinced me I should try it. I did. I didn't think I'd get hooked seeing how needles always freaked me out, but I was strung out already.

"I was feeling guilty about running away. I was so lonely for Mom and so homesick. But I knew I couldn't come back. She would talk about leaving Bob every time I called but I knew she'd go back to him if she did. And I just couldn't take any more of that scene. It would be the same scene I left, with Bob and Mom fighting all the time, her talking about leaving or leaving and then getting back together.

"So I was more unhappy than I'd ever been in my life. I was thinking about killing myself.

"In a way, the drugs were good for me. They gave me something to live for. Once I got hooked, every day I could think about how I was going to get my dope for that day, and I didn't have much time to feel miserable about anything else.

"And after awhile I even began to love needles. When I'd shoot up I'd leave the needle in my arm longer than I needed to because it was just a good kind of sensation. Sort of sexual, if you know what I mean.

"One thing I got to say about H. It's a great cure for desperation. At least, temporarily.

"At first Indio and his friends made no demands on me. They were selling enough drugs to pay the rent, buy the little bit of food we ate, you don't want much food when you're on scagg, and the H. we needed.

"Then one day Ariel, one of Indio's friends, said she wanted to talk to me.

" 'Listen, kid,' she said, 'I know you must feel bad not having any money to spend on yourself. I make one hundred dollars a night, the easiest money I ever made in my life. Maybe you'd like to go in business with me.'

"I asked her what kind of business she was in. She laughed and said, 'Hooking, of course. But it's not the way you think it is. It's sort of just dating lots of different guys. They call me for dates. I make about five or six dates a night, and each of them gives me at least twenty dollars. Actually, they're all nice guys and I'd be doing it with them, anyway. But this way I earn my living doing something I enjoy.'

" 'Anyway, things are going very well now, and I'm getting more calls than I can handle. So, since you're Indio's girl and he's one of my best friends, I thought about you.'

"At first I was shocked. I'd known Ariel awhile and had no idea she was a prostitute. She was the first one I'd ever met. And, of course, I soon met lots more. Most women on H end up hooking after awhile.

"Ariel told me to think it over. I asked Indio what he thought about it, and he said it was up to me. But I could tell he'd be very glad not to have to worry about money any more. So eventually I told Ariel I'd try it.

"In the beginning I was scared, nervous. I felt embarrassed, terrible. But Ariel was a big help. She introduced me to some of her men. And at first we'd even double-date.

"It was true I was making around one hundred dollars a night. I bought myself some beautiful clothes, really sexy, some good perfume, and nice jewelry. And the men treated me very well. It was no hassle. Never had any trouble getting paid or anything. I used to wonder who would I rather be, the cat's wife sitting home in some big house or me, the chick he was going out with. And I knew I was having the best time. I made some good friends with the Johns. They'd do me all kinds of personal favors, buy me jewels, perfume, fur stoles, dresses, shoes, or drive me wherever I wanted to go.

"The only real problem was the fact that the more money I made the more Indio and I spent on H. And after awhile we were spending about ninety dollars a day on the shit and I had to work whether I felt like it or not. On bad days when I didn't get enough calls from regular customers I even had to go out on corners. I didn't dig that at all. Standing in the rain or the cold wearing only short pants or dresses was really hell. But when you got a habit, you'll do anything. I had one other little problem with Indio. He was jealous as hell. Not of the Johns. As I said, he was glad I was working. He needed the H and he'd never worked in his life. Never done anything legit, that is. He used to rob people from time to time.

"He knew when I was with the Johns, it was business. But one night he came home and found me in bed with one of his friends. He freaked out. He grabbed the butcher knife and threatened to kill me.

"We finallly calmed him down and got the knife away from him. But then he said he was leaving. I had to cry and beg and plead for hours before he agreed to stay with me. After that I never went to bed with any of his friends, or anyone else who wasn't paying.

"Naturally I always used birth control when I was working. But Indio and I never used anything. I was only fourteen when I started trying to get pregnant. I don't know why it was so important to me. Maybe I was just trying to pay Mom back for having me when she wasn't married. I didn't think so at the time.

"I kept thinking a baby would be something to live for. And Indio told me his parents had a big farm in Puerto Rico, where we'd live when we both got straight. I thought if I had a baby, we could take it to the farm and raise it there.

"So I kept trying to get pregnant for two years. I worried about never being able to have a baby. I kept asking all my girl friends. Some of them told me that when you're on drugs it's hard to get pregnant, so I shouldn't worry. Once I stopped messing with narcotics, they assured me, I'd be able to have a baby.

"Anyway, after trying for two years, I decided I must be sterile. So I stopped using anything ever, even when I was working.

"When I found out I was pregnant, I felt all mixed up. I had no idea who the father was. He could be white, black, puerto Rican, Indian, Chinese. But I was relieved to know I could get pregnant and I never once considered abortion.

"Lots of the girls tried to talk me into having an abortion, since I didn't know who the father was. I reminded them how long I'd been trying to get pregnant. They kept saying I was only sixteen, a kid myself. But I knew that if I did get an abortion and later on couldn't get pregnant again I'd never forgive myself. So I never paid any attention to the abortion talk.

"Right away I got into a methadone program, told the doctor there I was pregnant and wanted to be cured as soon as possible. The idea of the baby was enough to help me get clean. But I was very weak from two years on drugs and I've had a hard pregnancy. I was sick from the beginning.

"Indio kept nagging me to go out on the streets to get the twenty dollars a week we needed for methadone, and our food and rent money. It wasn't much to earn. But I was so sick all the time I didn't feel like it, not even once a week.

"Indio and I fought all the time. He was convinced the baby was his, and he was worried about how we'd raise it. He tried hard to be good to me, but I was always in a bad mood because I felt so terrible, and he was uptight about getting bread. He needed more methadone than I did, and money was really getting tight.

"Finally he tried to rob a grocery store and got caught and sent to prison for a year. That's when I decided to come back home.

"I really love Indio. But I don't want to get back on drugs after I have the baby. So I'm not going to write him or his friends. He doesn't have my home address. So I guess I'll never see him again."

Having Cindy back gave Mavis the strength to get a separate apartment for herself and her daughter. She continued to see Bob, but living apart helped her to solve most of her previous problems. Later, when the baby was born, Mavis quit her job and went on welfare so that she could take care of the little boy while Cindy finishes school.

Cindy told me she's glad she has the child, whom she named R
ONALD% "I know I'll never go back on drugs," she told me. "I want to
be a nurse so I can support Ronald and myself. I want to give him a good
home. I know I couldn't be a good mother on drugs. So that's a part of
my past."

Mavis is proud of her grandson. She looks good, better than ever.
She's even taking education courses at night school so that she can
eventually become a teacher.

Maybe they'll finally be able to break the vicious cycle that messes up
lives. They are certainly trying. Like mother, like daughter, they say, but
you can break the curse. How wrong it is to type the young, the strange,
the temporarily deranged. These young girls are not merely vacant bodies
possessed by transient males with fantasies of ownership. Even when
enslaved by circumstances and convenience, they can break out of their
pattern to leave the street and the harshness of contemporary nomadic
life and touch home base.

Their goal always, after running away, is to establish their own centers,
to be self-supportive once they emerge from the fog precipitated by
sudden entry into the changing, brutal, and highly sexed society that is
ours.

6
Solomon

In 1965, my old man and I went to Morocco for a year. One day, after we'd been there for several months, Omar, an Arabian friend of ours asked us to go to Tangiers with him. He'd met a very nice American couple that he said reminded him of us. The man was a writer and his wife an artist. They were expecting their first baby.

We agreed to go with him. In Tangiers, Omar led us into the Medina, the Arabian section and the oldest part of town. We walked down the winding narrow paths lined with spice parlors, leather shops, tiny street cafes, past veiled Arabian women selling wares, sewing, or cooking, and through the droves of children who seemed to be everywhere.

When we finally reached the very end of the Medina and the home rented by the American couple, we were surprised to see how large it was and that it was an old mansion by the sea.

We climbed the steps that led to the house, went inside and met Solomon and his wife Jewel. Solomon was tall and thin with very curly black hair, large panda-bear eyes, and a long, lean nose. He was wearing an Arabian djellabah and sandals. Jewel had lovely long red hair that curled in all directions. She had hazel eyes and pale, freckled skin. She, too, was wearing Arabian clothes.

They served us some sweet mint tea and Arabian honey cakes. Solomon talked incessantly, most of it extremely interesting, and he had a fascinating way of using his hands to draw pictures in the air of whatever he was describing. He showed us a letter he had received from Jack Kerouac that said Jack wanted to remain Solomon's friend, but that Solomon was not to visit him again in his home because of his crazy ways, "freaked my mother out."

Solomon showed us some of his poetry. It was really beautiful.

"Here's one I wrote on the lower East Side," he said. "It's called St. Mark's Place:

> It's the funeral procession of the children's crusade
> The gloomy, foolish costumes, the sameness of the faces
> The timeless characters for the stranded and the strayed

The twinkle, blink, and twittering of all the gay betrayed
Yes, the jest of the host are the guests and the ghosts
on St. Mark's Place.

All the venerable despots having earned a day of fun
Have returned to peddle garbage or disgrace
In the caverns and the tunnels where the bandits needn't run
To the eager lambs and sparrows branded, blinded by the sun
And the lost are the least where the frost is the feast on
St. Mark's Place.

At the unblue mausoleum and other resorts
Witless litanies are chanted to the pilgrims of space
Ancient rituals are played at, as well as other sports
While attendants plant omens and whisper false reports
But the grip of the groom steers the trip to the tomb
on St. Mark's Place.

Solomon was boiling over with nervous energy, couldn't sit still a minute, walked from place to place bringing us manuscripts he'd written, his favorite books, records, and the like. Being with him was a heavy trip.

Jewel was almost the opposite of Solomon. She sat quiet, smoking keuf, the Moroccan version of marijuana, and meditating. From time to time she spoke in a low, calm voice. She seemed perfectly at home with her impending motherhood, and when she did get up to bring us tea or more biscuits, her walk was amazingly graceful for someone in the last months of pregnancy.

Solomon told us his life story:

"I was born in Brooklyn, the original Immaculate Conception. My blessed mother took one look at me and said, "Jesus Christ, he only has one ball." The doctors swore the other ball would descend to keep the solitary sphere company, but as usual they were wrong. But I was still able to perform the proper functions to make my contribution to the introduction of genius into the world, as Jewel's lovely belly will testify.

"My worldly father was a Jewish merchant who made himself enough money to buy his family a respectable mansion and ran away with his goyim sales clerk.

"I killed my first victim, myself, when I was three and was reincarnated as a child genius. Straight A's in school, Einstein in math, and James Joyce or Henry James in English.

"Wrote my first poem at five. Spent my childhood days reading medieval poets when I wasn't writing.

"At fourteen, I got hold of Ginsburg's *Howl* and it turned me on to the nature of reality, the naked truth known only to three-headed babes and virgin whores.

"Mescaline was the means to my first breakthrough into nirvana, where I now rest. Ginsburg, Kerouac, and their friends turned me on to freedom and the only life that's on the road to here. So I ran away at sixteen. Met my beat heroes in the Village, traveled with them, paying my dues, learning the unlearnable, turning on myself, and arresting the entire world.

"I met Jewel in that no-man's land called the Village. She had run away because her parents were unseeing, unfeeling, unalive wealthy bastards. She ripped off her old man for a small fortune; you see, the only real thing about her creepy old man was that he didn't trust banks so he kept his stash in a cafe. She got into the one in his store and there she was, set for a temporary eternity.

"We decided to test the vibes on the other side of the ocean, so we took a freighter to Morocco where you now find us."

Solomon was seventeen at the time I met him, but there was a certain cynicism, a certain worldly-wise air about him that gave the impression of his being much, much older. Jewel was six months older than he was and she, too, in her way gave the suggestion of being quite mature.

The second visit we made to Solomon and Jewel was shortly after their baby, a little girl they named Alpha, was born.

They sent us a small note telling us about the birth and inviting us to come and meet her. "Come meet Alpha, a transcendental falling star, a crystal from the cosmos. Share her flaming vibrations."

"You should have been here for the birthing," Solomon told us. "It was like a second Creation. Stars danced overhead. The shepherds played symphonies.

"We had a festival, with joy for all. Jewel had the ceremony on the beach with the help of an Arab midwife. We all meditated, smoked our peace and love pipes, sang our Oms, and prayed her out."

"It was great," Jewel said proudly. "We invited all our friends from Tangiers, and had our big eternal moment on the beach so that Alpha could dig the sea, the stars, the sky, and see that there is something worth staying for."

"And I have another big announcement." Solomon said. "I have decided to become a world-famous musician. I am now writing the words for my songs that will enchant the jungles of deaf zombies.

"I am studying the guitar, and soon I will be the world's greatest music maker and I shall wander the streets of the earth making music for the ears that long to hear, opening those that have ceased to."

We didn't see Jewel or Solomon for several months after that, but Omar kept us informed about them. He was enthusiastic about Solomon's guitar playing, said he'd never seen anyone learn music so rapidly, but he was worried about the fact that Solomon was spending too much time smoking hashish. "Kef will make him lose his mind," Omar told us, "He smokes much too much and he smokes the part the Arabs usually throw away, the part that makes you a madman."

But hashish was not the only danger. It seems they had met some American hippies who were into heavy drugs and had begun to experiment. Jewel soon became hooked on heroin while Solomon couldn't get along without amphetamines after awhile.

The final visit we made to their home was a sad one. Jewel greeted us. She had lost weight, was very pale and looked harassed.

"Solomon is in the nuthouse," she said. "It was dreadful. He took an ordinary piece of paper and wrote on it. 'This is a check for ten thousand dollars,' and went from bank to bank trying to cash it and threatening to kill the bank clerks when they refused. Finally, he made enough racket that one clerk called the police and they had him committed.

"I went to the embassy and I'm trying to get him released, but so far no luck. The embassy is trying to arrange to have him shipped back to America, but they say they'll send him to another nuthouse there. I'm really worried about him."

I visited Solomon in the mental hospital in Tangiers. He was wearing a pair of light blue pajamas that were much too big for him and carrying a piece of a guitar that he pretended to play on.

"My savior come down from the sky to carry me away," he said, 'kissing my arms, my shoes, my legs. Redemption, at last." He smiled. "This concentration camp is wearing out my soul. Swing low, silver chariot, I am sole survivor, back-seat driver, supernova, Trooper Jehovaha. Roll over and out."

He, too, had lost weight, and did indeed look like a concentration-camp victim. He held up the piece of a guitar, "I am an electric quartet. The exigencies of space and time decimated my guitar. I stand suspended in air. I can't go up and refuse to come down.

"Alpha, alpha is my singer. The song of songs. Alpha is the joy come to glorify the worldly. And now a solo by my lead guitar, my right hand, the weird wizard, Django Chickenclaws. Lefty Linkin on bass, on rhythm. The left hand of the Lord. Your choice, the voice, Miss Alpha, Star of David, singing the songs of the late, lamented, completely demented Solomon."

He ranted on and on, sang his strange songs.

When I was leaving, he tried to come with me. One of the attendants stopped him. He began to shout, "Let my people go! I am thy Lord, thy goddamned dog. This is the voice, your choice, your last chance to save a destroyed universe! This is the end of the end."

The next time I saw Solomon was several years later, back in New

York. I ran into him in the Village. He was wearing Bermuda shorts, red and green socks, and sneakers. He had on three pairs of broken sunglasses piled one on top of the other and was carrying a guitar. He was a little more together than he had been when I visited him in the mental hospital. From time to time he would go into his abstract talk, but in-between he managed to fill me in on what has happened to him and Jewel and the baby since I last saw them.

"So ingratiated to see you recognize my impotence," replied Solomon. "I am a potentially prestigious person on the verge of Godhood. I walk around in a corner of myself. One day I shall destroy the universe and recreate it with an invisible sphere of my halitosis. In the meantime would you kindly navigate me to the living room?"

Sarah blushed, realizing that Solomon was aware that she treated him as if he were helpless, or at least retarded.

But in a sense he was asking to be treated that way. He once searched for a small piece of hashish on a linoleum floor for three hours, forgetting after awhile what he was searching for. The floor had become the world and he was searching for treasure, the universe, the essence of life, the truth, the word that would make everything clear.

On one hand, I thought of him as being incredibly self-indulgent, because the connections are so much more difficult to discover, so much more tenuous, when you're not high and you're so much more vulnerable to the bullshit that passes for reality for most people. On the other hand, I thought of Solomon as a martyr, relinquishing life in order to unlock the treasure, liberate the essence, proclaim the word, and impart it to anyone who would listen.

He was always ready to share his wisdom: "I detest pockets. I am convinced that ultimately they will lead to fingerless, handless unhuman beings. Hands were meant to be free. Liberate your hands. Let your fingers fly. Pockets were the worst invention ever forced upon this poor unwitting world. The only other unsuccessful invention which can ever compare in its destructiveness is the automobile. When my position as Lord of the Universe is ultimately recognized, you will see the joys of a world without pockets, a world without cars. Amen."

And his songs and poems have real beauty. Here's one he handed me as I left Vermont:

Street flowers breaking through the sidewalk
Blooming in a valley of concrete and steel
Driven by the power that turns every wheel.
Street flowers reaching from the shadows
Riding the reflections in crystal and glass
Carrying a message: This too, shall pass.
Delicate petals sprang without warning

Came to deliver blessings of the morning.
Street flowers decorate the city
Blooming in the valleys of concrete and steel
Driven by the power that turns every wheel
And the flowers reveal
It is the power to feel.

That's how I see Solomon now, as one of his own street flowers. I still run into him from time to time, roaming the streets of the Village and the lower East Side. He's never without his faithful guitar, or his little bag of speed equipment, or the "works," as he calls it.

"Death is the final fix, using God's works," he told me once. And he seems to be speeding toward that.

Yet, he carries with him his messages of life. His philosophy of life and death are unique, as this last poem shows.

The skin is reticent,
But the flesh is raw
As always, superficialities prevail.
Denial is acceptable when consistent
But yet more enlightening when irrational.
Burglars work at night.
But freedom is timeless.
And what of the moon?
Einstein is unborn.
Vestiges dominate crises.
Rhythm could do it but who cares?
Still, rivers do not
Cease to flow by whim
Even if other things do
And knowledge, not control,
Follows perception.
Trump my ace.
I'll not renege.
Even as Job,
The Classic Fool
I'm no water walker
But I swim
If you drown
I'll swim harder.

7
Little Bit

This is mostly about Little Bit and her friends and the situations they got themselves into. It also reveals more about crash pads in the East Village, and how they multiplied in the late sixties to become home to the thousands of displaced youngsters rearranging the American dream.

Many of these pads were in the most rancid tenements on the raunchiest blocks, where the landlords were never choosy about their tenants. Storefronts, exempt from the city's regulations and rent-control laws, were especially popular.

Of course, there were exceptions, but still there were no rules for plumbing and ventilation. The landlord didn't care. He knew he was dealing with kids who couldn't complain to the authorities. He capitalized on that. He was always on the lookout for the highest bidder. And he'd raise the rent beyond the tenant's pocket. Runaway roulette. Somehow it got paid, or it didn't and eventually the inhabitants found themselves back on the street.

My first visit to a crash pad was on one of those bitter January days in the "Far East," when one knows for certain that the universe as such is quite indifferent to one's plight. My bathtub had conked out, and my son Raphael and I knocked on the apartment door two doors down, hoping there would be a working tub we could use.

There was—in a kitchen occupied by six people seated around a rickety wooden table set against the wall. Used dishes and cups were scattered over its surface and a Baggie with a small quantity of marijuana was perched on one side.

The room was lit by a single candle which illuminated the smooth, clear-eyed faces of the six and flickered over the bodies of three Siamese cats as they leaped into view from time to time.

The cats seemed to be having a better time of it than the people, whose conversation was minimal and thoughts seemed submerged. They were intensely apathetic, spaced-out on the fringes of a kind of psychedelic alternative-culture fog.

The kitchen was also occupied by hundreds of unusually bold roaches, as though they too knew whom they were dealing with—inexperienced kids.

A couple at the other end of the storefront, shut off from view, argued loudly. Raphael and I bathed, thanked our hosts, and left.

One rainy night the following week, one of the denizens of the crash pad, whose name I learned was Spaceman, knocked on my door. "No one's there," he said, "and I'm locked out. I was wondering if I could spend sometime here."

I said he could. I made some chili for him, Raphael, and me.

Spaceman had become a runaway gradually. He had been coming to the East Village for weekends while attending high school in New Rochelle and had slowly become accustomed to the hardships of living in a crash pad. The trick, he told me, is to teach the body to sustain life on anything—or practically nothing—and to "behave" so minimally that people are uncertain as to what sort of consciousness—if any—functions behind the vacant stare.

Spaceman had learned these lessons almost too well. In fact, he spent a bit of time at my pad—eating, drinking, burning incense, listening to records—before he said anything that wasn't related to the immediate situation, such as, "Do ya wanna hear the Grateful Dead?"

When he finally began to tell me about his life as a runaway, however, it came in a rush.   "First I lived on Eleventh Street," he said, "with Scott and Scott's girl friend and Cricket. That was when I still had my Moroccan drums."

"Then things were less and less cool with Scott because of his girl friend. I started hanging out more and more on Ninth Street, but while I was still on Eleventh Street one day, Cricket brought in this whole bunch of people who had run away.

"I told Cricket that Scott and his girl friend didn't want them to stay, that it would be cooler if we all went to the place on Ninth Street. So we went there.

"More things were happening on Ninth Street than on Eleventh Street because there were more people going out and coming in. Two of the chicks staying there, Cristalis and Amber, would go uptown to be with rock groups. Then they would come back and whisper a lot to each other and to Midnight. And the three of them would whisper amongst themselves and yell at Maurice.

"They would yell at Maurice when he came onto them. Maurice was always coming onto the three of them, so they were always yelling at him.

"In the evening, I would hang out around the Fillmore. Once I saw the Jefferson Airplanes. I saw other groups, too. But usually I was broke, so I just hung out outside looking at all the cute young chicks. I usually never got into anything with the ones who went inside, because if they didn't have dates when they went inside, I'd lose them. Them inside, me outside.

"But there were other chicks who would hang out outside, unless they could hustle some dude into taking them into the concert. Mostly the chicks who hung out outside were younger and didn't quite know what to do. Some of them would stick with another chick that they'd come with. I mostly got into raps with chicks who were alone. Sometimes they'd come back to the pad with me. They usually didn't stay very long. A couple of days, most of them. Sometimes they'd get freaked out and I just couldn't deal with it, so I'd split for a few hours and when I'd return, they'd be gone.

"Little Bit stayed longer than the others. She had split from her parents' home in Maryland, and then gone to visit her sister in a boarding school, and from there, she'd come to New York.

"She would get involved in a conversation with some dudes on the block, and they would be hassling her, and she didn't know how to get out of it and she expected me to do something about it, which I wasn't into. I tried to tell her that she herself had to deal with situations and she'd get pissed off, or if I split for awhile she'd be uptight about that, too.

"So finally I just couldn't dig what she was laying on me and I told her so, and she went back home."

The population of the crash pad was incredibly transient. Two months after my first visit, it was occupied by Spaceman, Dave, a gentle, skinny redhead who studied pre-med at Cooper Union and who was the official tenant and Om, a strikingly handsome black runaway, and a tattered urchin who made strange symbolic line drawings on the dismal walls of the storefront.

I dropped in early one afternoon when my son Raphael was with my sister. I was rather preoccupied that day because her eight-year-old son Jon had been attacked by a teen-ager at the boys' club who had literally ripped off his beads and almost choked him.

I began rapping to Spaceman, telling him how Jon was bored just coming home after school every day and had discovered the Church of All Nations' After-School Group. I had just passed the denoument about how Jon finds refuge and exercise on Second Street with two of his best friends, when I noticed a young girl sprawled on a chair in the corner, half hidden by the shadows.

I can't say why exactly, but somehow I knew that Little Bit had returned. I wondered how things would work out this time. It seemed romantic to me that she had come back to the East Village and found her long-lost love after six months.

I asked her a few casual questions, like where she was from, and whether she had noticed any changes since the last time she was in New York. She replied in monosyllables. Spaceman just kind of grunted.

I left, depressed by the emotional bleakness of the scene.

When Spaceman came over to my place four days later, he implied that things were going pretty much as they had before. He was feeling restless because Little Bit was almost completely dependent on him for stimulation, and Spaceman was the kind of guy who liked to spend a lot of time inside his own head.

Little Bit came over a couple of hours later, just as twilight was beginning to set in. We listened to a Buffalo Springfield album, spinning tinnily on my tiny Victrola. A joint was passed around and Little Bit was more talkative this time.

"I really like to get stoned," she said. "That's one thing I can't do at home. Actually, my parents aren't ogres. Just boring.

"They don't understand things. They think if you have a nice home, with all the appropriate gadgets, and a car and a grill in the backyard, then everything's just fine.

"They're not real strict with me. I can have dates and go to parties. But I feel it's so limited.

"The kids don't understand, either. They think it's a big deal if you're on the football team, or a cheerleader; and they can't wait to get a driver's license and drive the family car. That's supposed to be the living end.

"I mean all those things are okay; but there's got to be something more to life. For one thing, sex. If I sleep with a boy back home, either I have to go steady with him, which is practically like being engaged, or I'm a tramp and all the boys think they have a right to sleep with me, and the girls won't have anything to do with me—unless I act contrite so they can feel sorry for me.

"When I left home the first time, I stayed with my sister at her boarding school for awhile. I liked being there. I mean, the boarding school is okay. They don't have to work that hard, and they ride horses and have a swimming pool. And I liked being with my sister and her friends better than being at home.

"We even smoked some grass when I was there. Some girl had gone home for a weekend and managed to get some. We had to be really careful about smoking it, though. I mean any of the girls who go there would get expelled if it was discovered. And my sister said some of the girls—not her friends, of course—were snitches. Anyhow, we smoked it in the bathroom with the window wide open. It was freezing and everyone was very panicky and kept yelling for everyone else to shutup.

"Me, I'd rather relax when I smoke. Also I asked my sister if she didn't mind being in a place where there weren't any boys. And she said no, not really, that boys were just troublemakers as far as she was concerned, and she didn't want anything to do with them.

"I visited my sister this time, too, before I came to New York, but I was only there a few hours this time because the time before the people at the school had been upset about my staying there, though they did suggest that my parents have me enrolled there but I didn't want to.

"Anyhow, my sister gave me money to come up here both times, a lot of which was borrowed from the other girls. She said she didn't want me to hitch-hike because I'd probably get into trouble. I guess she's right. Anyhow, I came up here on the Greyhound both times."

Spaceman sat there mute. We didn't know whether he was inside his head or simply silent and listening. Little Bit would look at him, obviously trying to evoke a response. By the time the fourth joint went around, Little Bit was silent and looking anxious.

I asked her how she felt.

"I'm just fine," she said. "I've smoked grass lots of times and it doesn't bother me at all."

Her defensive tone reminded me of myself at about her age, nonchalantly choking on my third cigarette. But, aside from the difference in the smoke, I was a schoolgirl at thirteen, whereas this girl was attempting to master independence in a hurry. She was facing the dilemma of an adult, and having difficulty riding it out.

I tried to radiate the sympathy I felt, but by this time she was shut off from me. She only wanted some response from Spaceman, who wouldn't give her any. Little Bit split.

About five minutes later it flashed through my mind that, with her limited experience, she might be unprepared for the vicissitudes of the East Village at night.

"Hey, Spaceman," I said, "That's not never-never land out there. It's Avenue C. Maybe you ought to go look for her."

Spaceman left reluctantly and came back two hours later, saying he'd searched the neighborhood but couldn't find Little Bit.

We didn't see her until nine the next morning. Little Bit, he learned, had felt better once she was outside. She first considered her alternatives. She obviously wasn't making any headway with Spaceman, so it would be stupid to hang around. She'd find something else to do.

Maybe if she stayed out, he'd wonder what happened to her. She decided to check out Washington Square Park. During her last visit to the city, she'd heard a lot about the place but had never seen it.

She strolled over to St. Marks Place. She was smiling. Some people smiled back, some scowled at her menacingly. Most simply maintained their original expressions, and appeared not even to notice her. She tried to change that with good vibrations.

There was a big crowd in front of the building that housed the Dom and the Electric Circus. Several insinuating comments, shouted or hissed, came her way. She tried to figure out which invitation had been made by which grinning, smirking, or leering face.

When she reached the west side of Eighth Street, Little Bit wasn't sure exactly how to get to the park. She walked over to two men who were standing and talking in front of the bookstore, and asked them how to get to Washington Square Park.

"We're heading in that direction. Why don't you come with us?" replied the shorter of the two, who had flowing shoulder-length hair and incredibly large, sad eyes. His voice was gentle, like a caress.

Little Bit decided to go along with them.

"Why do you want to go to the park, anyway?" asked the one with the flowing hair, whose name turned out to be Spider.

"Because I'm new in town and I've never been there before. I heard about it, so I decided to check it out."

They walked under the arch, Little Bit between the two men. It was a clear, chilly night. You could smell the coming springtime in the air, but the temperature was still down in the low forties and the park was nearly empty. People passing through, but nobody was hanging out.

Little Bit thought the park looked like a stage set, although it was smaller than she had anticipated. She hoped she could make it some sunny Sunday afternoon to catch the show.

They went to Lee's house, a storefront on Prince Street across Houston, and stood around the stove while Lee, the taller of the two men, made coffee. Lee was muscular and wiry, with a shock of sandy-colored hair that feel over is glasses.

Spider addressed Lee, "Have you gone back to Cooper?"

"No," Lee said. "I didn't think it was really helping. I still draw and paint sometimes. But I'm more into structure, things like carpentry and plumbing. "I'm helping someone to construct the inside of a loft. Sort of interior architecture. When we started, the loft was just like a shell. And I've got lots of plans for this place."

He spread his arms to encompass the entire storefront, which was as long, and about twice as wide as Spaceman's on Avenue C, and in much better condition.

"I'm going to put in a lighting system. Lights will be coming up from behind wooden slates all around the place. Then I'll get a bunch of plants, construct a drainage system...."

Little Bit looked around the room, which was full of scraps Lee had picked up from the street. There lay about mountains of wooden planks, steel cylinders of varying lengths and widths—the sort that seem to be spewed up from the bowels of the city from time to time—and enough nails, bolts, screws, and other, more esoteric little pieces of metal to stock more than one hardware store.

"You're more ambitious than me," said Spider. "All I've been doing is stretching canvases for that dude on Fourth Avenue. Oh, yeah. Last week I made a sort of diorama, about this big." He demonstrated the size of the diorama by placing his hands about a foot apart.

"If I know Spider," Lee said, addressing Little Bit, "it's probably a masterpiece."

"You can come over later and decide for yourself," replied Spider. "Right now I've got to split."

Spider disappeared through the door, with catlike movements. Little Bit was disappointed. She'd really been attracted to Spider, much less to Lee.

But she didn't want to go back to the crash pad yet, and Lee seemed like an okay person to spend sometime with. Little Bit realized that she wasn't stoned any more, and felt that things would go better if she were.

"Do you have anything to smoke?" she asked Lee.

"I've got something better," he said. "Spider gave me some acid. I tried some a couple of nights ago. It's really sweet, not rocky. More like a light dose of mescaline, or some really good grass."

Little Bit had never had acid before. She was a bit frightened but figured if others survived it she would, too. She was excited as well as scared. Everyone had told her about how fantastic everything looked when you were tripping, and how great music sounded. She would try it out.

Lee pulled the cover off a small cylindrical plastic container and poured two tabs of acid into the palm of his hand. He turned on the faucet, swiping the water with his hand til it got cold enough.

They dropped the acid, like aspirin, with two or three gulps of water apiece, and sat around smoking brown hashish from a ceramic pipe while they waited for the acid to hit.

"What would you like to do tonight?" asked Lee.

"I don't know exactly," Little Bit answered. "Be nice to hear some live music."

"Know of any concerts?" asked Lee.

"No," she shook her head.

"Have you eaten yet?" he inquired.

"No."

"How about going to Max's Kansas City for dinner? Then we could go upstairs and dance. They have live music."

"That sounds far out," said Little Bit.

As Little Bit mused about what it would be like to go dancing in a night club, something she had never done, the acid hit with a bang, pulling her back to the room and an overwhelming awareness that there wasn't a single comfortable place for her to rest either her eyes or her ass.

Little Bit's head was spinning. She just has to sit down on whatever was available because she couldn't maintain her balance standing up. She'd never been so zapped.

Little Bit felt trapped. She didn't feel steady enough to leave alone, and she didn't really want to stay here with Lee. His expression challenged her. He had a "go ahead and show me something" look.

She knew that he'd realized she was disappointed when Spider left, that he'd probably tried to overlook it, but was dealing with it now.

Finally, after staring at Little Bit for sometime, Lee appeared to have made a decision. He stood up, stretched, and began to move toward Little Bit.

She rose to meet him. The floor seemed to her to be very far away. It was composed of millions of minute particles, and there was a pattern to their perpetual motion, which was infinitely complex.

The various pieces of lumber and scrap iron began to disintegrate, then recompose into one oppressively solid mass.

Little Bit clung to Lee for protection from the encroaching harshness of the environment. Then she realized that the harshness was an expression of Lee or part of him. Perhaps she could separate the two.

She was aware that the acid was intensifying both her perceptions and her emotions. It didn't matter. She had no real desire to turn away from this new, awesome reality. It was as if she, like Alice, had disappeared through a looking-glass and on the other side was another world that this, paradoxically, was only a shallow reflection of. The perception was terrifying but at the same time made more sense than ever before.

Little Bit had a quick succession of realizations about Lee. Lee assumed that women did not desire him and was angry at them on that account. He longer for a miracle, for her to want him.. Yet, he arranged everything—the place he lived in, his appearance—so that he was unappealing. Maybe, if they were somewhere else, she could bring him up. They could feel good together.

Little Bit could feel pulses beating all over Lee's body, and the pressure of his body against hers made her aware of the hammering of her own. She could not distinguish between them.

"Lee," she whispered, "Let's go over to the East Side. Probably no one's at the place where I'm staying. There's lots of soft places to lie down, and a bunch of incense, and three groovy cats, two black ones and a calico.

"Or, we could go to Maryanne's next door. It's comfortable there, too, and she's got some far-out records...." Little Bit's voice trailed off. She could feel Lee's body harden against here. She had felt muscle before; now she was more aware of the basic skeletal structure.

Lee took Little Bit by the shoulders and pushed her slightly away from him. His eyes narrowed. "Don't create problems," he said. "We're going to stay here. Here is just fine. If you're tired of standing, we can go lie on the bed. It's on the other side of the partition."

Little Bit sighed. She knew it wouldn't be easy to get Lee to leave with her, that he would be defensive. "That's what being hung-up is," she thought, "being unable to separate yourself from things you must be aware are unappealing, having to defend negative things instead of sloughing them off."

Little Bit wasn't exactly surprised when Lee wanted to make love. She really didn't want to, but strangely, it didn't seem like an especially important matter for resistance. It was more a matter of time. She would have to get him to leave with her before long, or leave alone.

It wasn't really a bed, more of a broad bench or another level of floor, that Lee had constructed. No mattress. Nothing really soft and cushy in the whole damned place. Their bodies were awkward together. Lying down, and getting undressed was an exceedingly complicated project.

After they had undressed, and were lying down beside each other, Lee began to manipulate her breasts. Her nipples became harder and tender. When it began to hurt, she pushed his hand gently away. She began to rub his body. And he began to massage hers.

Since she couldn't relate to it sexually, it was merely irritating, so she pulled his hand away and climbed on top of him. In this position, she could use his cold, suspicious glances to her advantage. But he would not let her remain on top. Underneath Lee, Little Bit felt as if she were being drilled by something mechanical, a programmed automation. She couldn't wait for it to end.

Little Bit felt drained when they finished. She sat there and watched, as Lee went over to the sink and poured a glass of water for them. By the time he returned with the glasses, Little Bit recovered enough strength to say, "Will you come with me now?"

"I'll think about it," he said curtly.

Lee was sitting on the toilet he'd installed—the throne, you might say. Little Bit was still desperate to leave as soon as possible. She asked, pleaded, cajoled, and finally, almost dragged Lee off the toilet and out into the street.

She hadn't even given him a chance to remember to put on a jacket, and it was a cold day in November.

The lights on Bleeker Street seemed to be blinking. This cheered Little Bit. She began to anticipate whatever was going to happen next with a pleasurable abandonment.

Lee hailed a cab, which, surprisingly enough, actually stopped in front of them, that is, they half felt that they were invisible to everyone who wasn't on their trip, and it seemed kind of amazing to have made connection with the Chinese cabbie.

This led Little Bit to hallucinate jasmine wafting toward her through balmy air. The driver appeared not to understand English, at least not their English, which was rather to be expected.

Lee and Little Bit despaired of making him understand exactly where they wanted to be let out. They settled for Avenue A, which left them two long, cold, desolate blocks to walk. They argued over who should wear Little Bit's smooth skimpy fur jacket. Little Bit let Lee have it for awhile, then grabbed it back, planning to let him have it again after she had warmed up.

Lee stopped walking when they were approaching the crash pad.

"I'm not going home with you," he said.

"Then I'll go home myself," Little Bit replied sharply.

Lee held Little Bit's keys. She'd given them to him because neither her black velvet pants nor her gray fur jacket had any pockets.

"Could I have my keys?" She asked.

Lee took the keys from his pocket, threw them up into the air in front of Little Bit's face, and caught them.

He hid his hand behind his back and laughed harshly.

He turned away from her and walked into some doorway.

Little Bit followed him.

He was covered with blood and vomit. Little Bit didn't know where the blood had come from.

She ran to the door of the crash pad for help. She knocked, then pounded on the door several times. She became involved in the motion of her arm and hand and the sound of her knuckles against the wooden door. She was banging out a primitive rhythm, a coded message.

Someone from an apartment upstairs yelled, "Shaddup!"

Little Bit began to look around waiting for what would happen next.

A thin, sallow-skinned youth emerged from the darkness. "Are you all right?" he asked. His voice was surprisingly tender, close. He had a slight Spanish accent.

"Somebody took my keys, and no one's home so I can't get into my house," said Little Bit.

"I'm going to my sister-in-law's," he said. "Do you want to come with me?"

"Yeah," she answered.

It seemed like a reasonable place to be. There was carpeting on the floors, a couple of deep chairs, and a sofa. The colors were pure and intense—bright reds, greens, and turquoise, palpable colors that made Little Bit shiver until she got into their velvety warmth.

Drums and other musical instruments in cases were stacked in the archway between the living room and the bedroom.

"Who plays those?" asked Little Bit.

"Me and my brothers and some friends," said the youth, whose name was Jesus.

There was a man asleep on a cot in the bedroom and a man and a woman on a king-size bed that dominated the bedroom, which was separated from the living room by an archway and partially hidden from view by a beaded curtain.

Little Bit sensed rather than saw the movement of the man and woman under the blankets. The woman giggled, a nice rippling sound.

Jesus opened up the sofa and he and Little Bit lay down on it. He pulled her toward him. She felt suffocated and pulled away, saying she needed room to breathe. She felt that her chest could easily be crushed.

"Don't push me," said Little Bit.

"I wasn't pushing, I was pulling. What do you want to do?"

"Talk. Tell me a bedtime story."

"What kind do you like?"

"Tell me about you. Do you live with your brother?"

"Yes. I started living here a few months ago."

"Where were you before that?"

"Nowhere. Out on the street. I was an addict."

"Did you break into people's houses and disappear into the night with their TV's and stereos?"

"No. I was more into mugging. If I'd met you out on the street at night a few months ago, I would have crept up behind you like a cat, then before you could react to my presence I'd have had my arm around your neck. I would have taken everything you had."

"Then you must have wasted a lot of time. I don't have anything."

"I was also into con games."

"Like what?"

"I'd look for Johns looking for women. I'd tell them I had a woman for them. They'd follow me into a building, and somehow I'd get his money from him and leave him there, waiting for me to come back with the woman.

"Sometimes I got him to let me hold his money on the grounds that there were too many rough characters around who might take it before he had a chance to spend it.

"Sometimes I'd put his money in a sealed envelope, like that was the way he was supposed to give it to the woman. Just in case there was a cop around, it would be safer for her that way. Then I'd exchange envelopes on him."

"Did you ever wish you could see the cat's face when the realization dawns on him?"

"Yeah, but I wanted my fix more."

"What made you stop?"

"I almost O.D.'d. I was becoming more and more paranoid. Different things. Smashing my cool. I got on methadone. I'd like to get off that, too. It's harder than getting off junk in a way because it's so easy."

"You're lucky you have a brother you can stay with."

"Yeah, he's a good man."

Jesus pulled Little Bit to him. They kissed for a long time. One movement melted into another until Little Bit was having a continuous orgasm, which she loved until she began to be afraid it would never stop.

Jesus was finished but Little Bit's body kept on going. She held her knees to her chest. She began to feel nauseous.

Jesus was puzzled. "Aren't you going to sleep?"

"No. I'm tripping and I feel restless."

She got up to go to the bathroom. All the lights were out so she left the bathroom door open a crack.

Two voices whispered, "Shut the door," not exactly in unison. She couldn't imagine why there couldn't be just a crack of light, and stood there awaiting an explanation. She noticed four cats at her feet. They fled.

"Don't let the cats out," one of the voices continued, "because of the pigeon."

Little Bit heard a weak flapping of wings against cardboard, and followed the sound. She understood when she saw the wounded pigeon in a box; they were trying to nurse it back to health and the cats would eat it if allowed to roam around.

She shooed the cats back into the bathroom and followed them in. She couldn't bear the total darkness. The cats were a representation, a replica, of the human scene on the other side of the door.

There were three males, all of them black, gray, and white. The one female had orange and white stripes and there was a bell around her neck.

Little Bit finally emerged from the bathroom, resigning herself to the darkness. She brought with her to the couch a bowl in case she had to throw up, an ashtray in case she wanted to smoke, and a glass of water in case her throat got dry.

She tried to find a comfortable position on the couch but failed. She went back to the bathroom and returned with another bowl, ashtray, and glass of water in the event she couldn't find the other ones.

She repeated the deed until the couch was completely surrounded by most of the dishes in the house.

Meanwhile, the three men fell asleep and the woman, who was either an insomniac or curious about her strange uninvited guest—or both—arose from her bed, covered her voluptuous body with a robe, and thrust her feet into slippers.

She ensconced herself in one of the plump armchairs facing Little Bit. The girl was perched on the floor, huddled on one leg, her scrawny wings enclosing her other leg and torso. She focused on the woman's legs in front of her. They were muscular and shapely.

The woman's melodious voice had a slight, almost-indeterminate foreign accent. "Are you all right?"

"Yeah, I've been tripping. Acid. I'm on the down side now. Things are falling into place now. Where are we? I mean, what street are we on?"

"Tenth between B and C."

"I live on the other side of the block, Ninth between B and C. I had no idea where I was."

It was a cozy world, even better now that the dawn was beginning to seep in around the edges of the curtains.

"Have you lived around here long?" Little Bit asked.

"For over a year. Before that I lived on 110th Street with my aunt and uncle. I was born in Puerto Rico, but my aunt brought me here when I was a baby. She kidnapped me from my parents because she couldn't have children of her own, and she and my uncle had always wanted children.

"When I got married last year, my husband said that as a wedding present we would go to Puerto Rico and find my parents. We searched for three months before we found them. Then we stayed with them for a month and came back here."

"How old were you when you got married?" Little Bit asked.

"Fifteen."

"That seems so young," Little Bit said. "I'm thirteen and I don't know if I ever want to get married."

"I don't think it's a matter of age," the woman said. "Some people would never be ready. I've been very happy with my husband. The only thing that bothers me is I've been married for two years and I haven't become pregnant. I'm afraid I'll be barren like my aunt."

When Little Bit left soon after, the woman insisted on giving her a quarter so that she could get some coffee. She had told her about being locked out of her apartment.

Out on the street, Little Bit realized she was still high, painfully sensitive to the putrid vitality of the garbage, the subtle hues and rough textures of the bricks, the nearness of the East River evident in the misty air. She was enmeshed in an inanimate, yet vibrant world.

She went to the luncheonette on Ninth Street and Second Avenue. The newspaper trade at the front window was slack. Inside, the store was surprisingly well-populated and bristling with tension.

A guy Little Bit had come to think of as "the blind hippie," the one who played the flute or sometimes the clarinet on the streets and left the case open for people to deposit change in, was sitting at one of the tables, his pale face contorted with pain. A tall, blond, shaggy-haired young man in a peacoat was bending over him.

"Get me some stuff," the blind hippie muttered urgently.

"I can't. I'm sorry. Try to cool down. You're just making yourself feel worse. Believe me, man I'd help if I could."

The shaggy-haired man departed, leaving several seconds of cold air in his place.

The blind hippie looked really desperate.

A tall, lean young black man in a black leather jacket walked over to him, sat across the table from him.

"Hey, baby," he said. "You've got to pull yourself together. You can get yourself all worked up, but it won't do you no good."

He reached over and put his hand on the blind hippie's arm but the blind hippie withdrew his arm and continued to fume.

The young black man sat at the counter, still gazing at the blind hippie. Suddenly, he whirled around on his stool and signaled the sullen-looking waitress, who as usual took her time about coming over.

The blind hippie was banging on the table, in rhythmic desperation, and cursing in a stage whisper. The large white-haired Russian who owned the place walked up behind the blind hippie, his mouth set firmly against any betrayal of sympathy or even pity.

"I know you're behing me," the blind hippie said. "You'd like to throw me out, wouldn't you? But you won't because I'm blind."

The Russian retreated, which dispelled much of the accumulated tension.

Little Bit went to one of the phone booths in the rear and called me. She explained the situation and I told her she could come over. "I hope you can sleep now," I told her. "I want to sleep for at least three more hours."

It was now sunny but still cold. Little Bit looked relieved when I answered the buzzer. I let her in and went back to bed, after showing her the sleeping bag, sheet, and blanket I'd left on the floor in the front room for her.

She lay there still awake and alert from the acid, though her body was exhausted, and was deep in thought when my four-year-old son Raphael came into the front room, surprised to have a visitor instead of a TV set to keep him company during the first hours of his day.

Little Bit asked him if there was any milk and he got it out of the refrigerator. They found the chocolate and she made them some chocolate milk.

They played with red glass beads, which they made into pictures first in a box top and then on the floor. The beads were so fluid, they reminded Little Bit of a kaleidoscope even through they were all one color.

Little Bit decided to take a bath. Raphael showed her where the light switch was, and she made the bath hot, wallowing in the heat that seemed to penetrate her pores, sooth her. She shampooed hair. She was washing everything out.

It was all falling down. All falling into place. Let Lee have the key. She'd get another. She had found the keys to herself. She was scrubbing her mind.

Another day would come. She would be here. She would continue. The streets would not change. She would continue to grow. To grow up. Slowly and wisely.

She put her head under water for an instant, and felt herself entering a whole other world of expanding light and galloping ecstasies.

Little Bit told me about her trip when I woke up later in the morning. "I feel so strange now," she said, "as though I had left myself on the trip. It's like I've been through a lifetime, birth to death. I'm so tired. I never felt more exhausted in my life, but my mind is still galloping along."

I assured her she'd feel better after she slept.

Little Bit lay down on the sleeping bag, curled in a fetal position. Her pale blue eyes stared straight ahead as she appeared to hypnotize herself to sleep. "Life is some trip," she mumbled before she finally allowed herself to sink into a deep slumber.

8
Bunny and Josie

I met Bunny on the express train running from Laredo to Mexico City. She was an attractive young woman with long honey-colored hair, stunning blue eyes with thick lashes, a classical Jewish nose, a uniquely sensual mouth, and a bright smile.

We exchanged pleasantries and struck up a conversation that continued throughout the trip. Bunny told me she was on her way to a small Indian village near the Guatemalan border, where she intended to do research for her master's thesis in anthropology.

"I've been there before," she told me. "It was seven years ago and it was a real nightmare scene for me at the time. When I left I didn't think I'd ever want to go back.

"But I'm much older now and I feel stronger and if the village is anything like I remember it, it's the perfect subject for my thesis."

She looked so young, I felt compelled to ask how old she'd been on her first visit.

"I was only fourteen. I ran away with my best friend Josie." She breathed a deep sigh, and began one of the strangest runaway adventures I'd ever heard.

"My friend Josie always seemed strange in a way, even though we were best friends for almost ten years and told each other most of our secrets.

"We were close almost from the time she moved into the neighborhood. Josie was two years older than I, but it felt like the other way around. I was Josie's protector from the other kids. Her family had come from Europe. They'd move around a lot. She'd learned to speak English before she came over here, but the kids thought her accent was funny. I think Josie would have been shy, anyway, but not speaking like the other kids intensified it.

"Josie came over with her mother. Her father had died when she was three. Josie and her mother moved in with her mother's aunt and uncle who lived down the block from us. The aunt and uncle seemed nice enough. No one ever said anything against them. But they were sort of stiff and kept pretty much to themselves.

"Anyhow, Josie and I spent a lot of time together playing jump rope, hide and seek, all the games kids play, and talking, incessantly talking.

"Josie had a vivid imagination and I always found the stories she made up fascinating. She especially liked stories about witches and witchcraft. Her stories usually included princes and princesses who were instructed by the witch in the making of spells and magic potions.

"Josie would become completely absorbed in her story. It was as if she thought that if she believed in her stories enough, they'd come true.

"Josie's mother was a worrier, just like mine, only worse. Probably the enormity of being solely responsible for the child exaggerated her natural tendencies. Josie's father had died of pneumonia, which gave her mother an excuse to be super uptight about any hint of illness. Josie spent a lot of time out of school because of this, and I envied her, although it was a drag the way her mother always nagged her about wearing a sweater or boots on warm, sunny days.

"It was weird about Josie's father, not the way he died, but the way her mother handled it. She never actually told Josie he'd died. She told her that her father had gone on a long journey.

"Josie told me that for years she actually believed her father would return, maybe as a reward for her good behavior. She said that when her mother first began to talk about coming to America, her first thought was that she would be reunited with her father.

"Josie's mother never actually admitted that the father was dead until she decided to remarry and that was the main reason for Josie's wanting to run away. I don't know if Josie was angry with her mother for having been dishonest with her all those years or for finally forcing her, because of the mother's own desires, to face the truth.

"Anyhow, the immediate circumstance which made Josie decide to run away was that her mother planned to remarry. Josie considered her mother's forthcoming marriage a betrayal of her father. She ranted and raved at her mother, was rude to her mother's fiance, and in general made life extremely difficult for her mother.

"So in order to make the period preceeding her marriage easier, and to assuage her own guilt feelings, which Josie had come to represent, she decided to send Josie to a boarding school. This proved to Josie that her mother didn't love her, and freed her emotionally to run away, maybe in search of the spirit of her father.

"From the beginning of the runaway plans, Josie and I both knew I'd go with her. But for me running away was simply a marvelous adventure and I didn't feel compelled to leave. And in the back of my mind was the assumption that I'd go home sooner or later."

Bunny's father was a lawyer with his own law firm in Philadelphia. He also owned enough real estate to insure the family an income for life.

Her parents, however, were always careful never to subject their children to any "hateful displays" of emotion—which, of course, led to the absence of any kind of emotion from the home, including affection, love, caring.

"As a young child," Bunny told me, "I did not dispute that my father was the superior being my mother made him out to be. I simply did not see what it had to do with me, or why she shoved his virtues down my throat like vitamin pills.

"My mother certainly did not encourage a real relationship between my father and me. She always said or insinuated that he was either too busy or too tired to pay any attention to me. And my father did nothing to counteract that impression."

So Bunny and Josie ran away.

"We took the Greyhound bus to San Francisco and went to Haight-Ashbury, where we made inquiries until we met some hippies who offered us a place to stay.

"After a week in San Francisco, we started to worry about being recognized as runaways. It began when we were entering a restaurant and I thought I saw Daddy.

"We tried to get away before he saw us, but Josie bent forward to look in the window and the man turned to face her. It wasn't Daddy. But the shock was too much for us and we realized how easily we might have walked into him. We made up our minds to hitch-hike to Mexico.

"We were lucky with rides. The first lift was with two attractive women heading for Los Angeles. After we'd ridden for an hour or so, the blond woman who was driving asked us, 'Are you two lovers?'

"At first neither of us understood the question. Then the second woman, who had beautiful red hair, put her arm around the driver, kissed her on the lips, and said: 'We are.'

"We got the point. 'We're best friends,' I told them nervously.

" 'How would you like to spend some time at our place in L.A.?' the driver asked.

" 'Thanks, anyway,' Josie told them, 'but we're in a hurry to get to Mexico.'

"In Los Angeles, the women let us out at what they said was the best stop to get a ride to Tijuana. We carefully chose a ride all the way to Tijuana with an elderly couple who told us they were on vacation.

" 'It's our first trip out of the country,' the woman said, 'We're very excited.'

"We had no trouble at the border.

"At Tijuana, we met a young American student who'd just come from the small Indian village in the Yucatan where he'd met most of the villagers and made friends with the chief. He told us we should go there if we got the chance. Since we had no direction in particular, we decided to go there right away. He gave us instructions as to how to get there, and wrote a note in Spanish for us to give the chief, telling him we were good friends of his.

"Life in that little Indian village was a beautiful experience at first. We'd never seen such lush foliage, such fantastic scenery; the rich blue skies day after day with a few pure white clouds sprinkled in interesting formations; the multicolored mountains with their fabulous jungle plants and trees.

"Indian women in bright handwoven native clothing sat at their weaving hour after hour, their entire presence peaceful, almost trance-like. Others walked to the river to do their laundry with baskets full of clothing on their heads. Still others stooped over carbon burners cooking meals. Half-naked, happy children roamed freely from hut to hut, confident that all adults were their relatives and would protect them from any harm.

"The Indian men squatted together to discuss the affairs of the tribe, or bent over leather, working and tanning it. There was a strong odor of fresh leather all about as the men made purses and sandals to sell to tourists in nearby villages.

"Harik, the Indian chief, saw to it that Josie and me received royal treatment. Every morning one of the single women in the tribe who was vying for Harik's attention would bring breakfast for him and Josie and me. Whenever we offered to help with any of the duties, he insisted we relax and enjoy ourselves. 'You are my guests,' he would say.

"I noticed that Josie was becoming more and more interested in the chief. And he seemed to feel the same way about her. From time to time I would watch them as their eyes met and they seemed to be sending each other intimate messages. I didn't know why, but it frightened me very much.

"One day, the chief had a strange, but very impressive visitor, an old Indian woman with a black shawl which was unusual since most of the shawls were woven in wild, frantic, glorious colors. This woman was dressed all in black. Her shawl covered her unruly gray hair except for the strands which fell on her face.

"Her back was stooped and her face was covered with deep wrinkles. Her eyes were piercing, reminding Josie and me of an eagle's eyes and giving us the uneasy feeling that she could read our minds and see into our very souls.

"She had a long beaked nose and a thin purplish mouth.

"Harik told us she was a bruja, and when we asked him to explain, he said, 'She uses herbs and prayers and spells to cure people or help them get something they want or protect them from the evil eye.'

"The bruja scared me and I tried to avoid her, but Josie was fascinated by her, stayed as close as possible to her. They had deep conversations that I couldn't understand since I didn't know much Spanish, but Josie's background in French and her aptitude for language enabled her to pretty much master enough Spanish to carry on conversations on almost any subject.

"The intensity of the conversations with the bruja really worried me. After she left, I questioned Josie about them.

" 'She's a wonderful wise old woman, Josie told me. She knows how to work magic and she likes me very much. She promised to show me how to make the chief fall in love with me.'

At first I thought Josie was joking, but her voice was too serious and the expression on her face said she was for real.

"The witch, as I began to call her, came back to the chief's very often after that on the premise that she was teaching Josie to speak the Indian dialect. Actually, she was schooling her in witchcraft.

"I didn't like it, begged Josie not to get involved with black magic, but Josie insisted this was not black magic but a special spiritual form of healing and helping people be happy.

"The witch told Josie how to cook sweat rice for the chief and said that once he ate it he would love her forever. She was to boil rice, and while it was still steaming, take off her underwear and sit over the pot, letting her sweat go into the rice while she repeated some Indian words the bruja taught her.

"Josie insisted on doing it. I tried to talk her out of it, but she was determined.

"Perhaps the spell worked. Josie was convinced it did. Anyway, shortly after that the chief asked her to marry him and be his number-one wife. He was careful to explain to her that he might take another wife or two later on, perhaps even me if Josie and I agreed, but that Josie would always be wife number one and have the say over which woman or women he could marry as well as other important matters.

"That conversation with the chief convinced Josie that she'd have to learn a lot more magic in order to keep the chief for her husband in a monogomous relationship, but she felt confident that the bruja would teach her everything she needed to know.

"Josie and the chief were married in a large spectacular ceremony. Everyone from the village came. It was a great fiesta with bright colors, dancing, and drinking posh, the special homemade brew that is stronger even than tequila.

"Josie seemed ecstatic. But I felt bewildered. What would Josie's mother say about the marriage? I had always felt Josie and I would return to Philadephia when we were old enough to be on our own in our family's eyes. But now it seemed like a different world, so far from this one and I just couldn't see either of us spending the rest of our lives in this little Indian village.

"Josie was so busy with her duties as the chief's wife and her studies of the language and customs of the tribe as well as her witchcraft that I felt very much alone and very homesick. I became more and more depressed.

"As Josie got deeper into witchcraft, her actions got more and more weird. She began wearing strange combinations of colors, lots of reds and purples, crimsons, bright oranges and yellows. 'My spirit wants me to wear them,' she'd tell me.

"Josie spoke more and more of her spirit. She'd give him various names, all Indian, and she'd talk about him as though he were a close friend or relative sharing her life. 'He wants me to burn incense.' 'He wants me to drink coffee.' 'He wants me to smoke a pipe.' 'He wants me to light a fire.' 'He wants me to throw freshly ground coffee all over the floor.'

"Her spirit was especially fond of coffee. This surprised me as much as anything because Josie had never liked coffee before we came to Mexico. She always preferred tea. Now she almost never drank tea, except when she'd mix strange herbs and make an evil-smelling broth which she drank, telling me her spirit had ordered her to.

"I asked her how her spirit spoke to her.

" 'We don't use words,' Josie said. 'It's sort of mind reading.' Josie had never seen her spirit, but she had felt him and she almost always knew what he wanted.

"One night I was awakened by bloodcurling screams coming from the room where Josie and the chief slept. At first I thought he and Josie were having a terrible fight. I could hear the sounds of physical fighting, but it was so out of character for the chief. He was always so calm, kind, and good-natured. What had Josie done to get him this upset?

"I jumped out of bed and slipped into my robe and started toward the master bedroom. Then I heard Harik's concerned voice, 'What's wrong, Josie? Are they after you? Ask them what they want. Whatever it is, we'll get it for them.'

"I wondered what in the world was going on. Who was in there attacking Josie? I threw open the door and couldn't believe my eyes.

"The chief, in his white sleeping clothes, was standing over Josie, who lay on the bed, being tossed from side to side as though an invisible force were picking her up and throwing her. She was moaning and screaming. Her face covered with scratches. The bedclothes were falling off the bed. The pillor was on the floor.

" 'What's going on?' I asked.

" 'Her spirit is fighting her,' the chief said. 'He wants her to do something for him. We must find out what he wants. Otherwise he may kill her.'

"I was stunned. I was afraid of magic, especially black magic. But I didn't really believe in it. And the chief was a scholar. He had studied at the University of Mexico. How could he believe in spirits? And yet what was happening to Josie certainly wasn't natural.

"Josie began shouting, 'No. I can't do that. I won't. I can't. Okay. I will. I will.' "

"Then she lay quietly, catching her breath. A few minutes later, she said in a weak voice, 'Please get me some perfume.'

" 'So that's what he wants,' the chief said. 'Many of them like perfume.'

"I thought they'd both gone mad. I felt I had to get out of there. But I couldn't leave Josie, not like that. I didn't know what to do.

"The chief calmly walked over to the little desk which held Josie's toilet items. He picked up a bottle of perfume she had received as a wedding present and handed it to her.

"She put it to her lips, and began gulping it down as through she'd been dying of thirst.

"I tried to grab it away from her. 'Don't, Josie. Don't drink that. It'll make you sick. It could kill you.'

" 'She has to drink it,' the chief said.

"Josie drank the entire bottle, and handed it empty to the chief. She lay for a moment staring at the ceiling before going into a deep sleep.

" 'Will she be all right?' I asked.

" 'She's fine now,' Harik assured me. 'Let her rest. She's had a hard night.'

"There were many similar nights after that when the sound of Josie fighting her personal devil woke me, but none as as frightening as that first one.

"Josie was always preparing evil-smelling combinations of herbs, putting them in a pot on the charcoal burner and leaving them to boil for days, constantly adding ingredients, stirring and mumbling her strange words. often carrying on conversations with her spirit.

"Most of Josie's spells were to help people get well. She had cured several people in the tribe and was getting a name as a spiritual healer, so that more and more sick people were coming to her.

"And whenever it seemed that one of the women in the tribe had caught Harik's interest, Josie would burn a special candle, drink some herb tea, speak her magic words, and soon the chief would pay no more attention to the girl.

"Josie was trying to convince me to go with her to the yearly meeting of the spiritual healers, which was to be held Friday at midnight. I told her I was afraid to go. Josie insisted that nothing would happen to me, said she just wanted me to be her assistant.

"When I absolutely refused, Josie got angry and said, 'You'll be sorry. I'll make you sorry.'

"That night I woke up feeling like something was crawling all over me. I got up and lit the candle next to my bed. I let out a scream when I saw two huge black rats clinging to my nightgown. When I tried to push them off, they'd leap to another part of my body. They ran down my neck, on my shoulders. I screamed until the chief came running to ask me what was wrong.

" 'It's rats,' I screamed. But when I looked down for them, they had disappeared.

" 'There are no rats here,' the chief said. 'We have cats who scare them away. You must be mistaken unless—' and his eyes grew wider.

" 'Unless what?' I asked him.

" 'Oh, nothing,' he said. 'You must have dreamed about the rats. You see there are none. Now you should try to get some sleep.'

"I lay there wondering if I had actually seen the rats. I was sure they were real. I couldn't have been dreaming. I wasn't asleep. Then I remembered how Josie had threatened to make me sorry for not going with her to the ritual.

"I dreaded going even more now, but I knew I'd have to go. What was happening to Josie? Would she really have done that to me, her best friend—if it were possible?

"I helped Josie catch a red rooster to take as her offering. The meeting was on the edge of the hill. There were many men and women, all dressed in vivid colors. Each had brought an animal to sacrifice.

"I held my eyes as one by one the animals were killed with various rituals, gutteral Indian words mumbled by the entire group and complicated drawings etched on the ground. They killed the animals over a huge wooden tub. They collected the blood and each of them took a bath in the blood after all the animals had been killed.

"Josie took her blood bath and begged me to take one, too. 'It's a protection from evil spirits,' she said. 'The evil eye is very strong here. You really must bathe. That's the main reason I wanted you to come with me. Because I love you and don't want anything bad to happen to you.

" 'It will protect you from *boodas,* people who can eat you with their eyes. There are lots of them in the tribe. They are sort of like psychic vampires eating your life force.' Josie looked very concerned. I thought she was going to cry.

"I wanted to take a blood bath to please Josie, but it looked so awful. I couldn't force myself.

"There were wild, ritualistic dances to the sounds of frantic, accelerating drumbeats that echoed through my head. Almost everyone danced, became possessed, shouting in strange tongues, hitting themselves, throwing themselves on the ground, or falling down, passing out, dancing on fire, eating fire or glass without getting hurt.

"I sat there numb, shivering, waiting for Josie to finish dancing and return to herself so we could go home.

"On the way back to the chief's house, I told Josie, 'I think we should go back to Philadelphia.'

" 'Sometimes I think so, too,' Josie confessed, 'but I don't think I could ever leave this place. I'll probably die here.'

"The way she spoke of dying I felt she meant soon, but I tried to ignore the feeling. 'Maybe we could go home for a vacation,' I said. 'You're married now and that makes you an emancipated minor. They couldn't force you to stay home.'

" 'That's not what I'm afraid of,' Josie said. 'I'm not the same person I was when I left. They'd probably put me in the nuthouse when they heard me fighting my spirit. Here it's accepted. It's natural. They know how to deal with it. It makes me special, gives me a certain respect. In Philadelphia I'd be crazy. You know that.'

" 'But you could leave all that behind you,' I told her.

" 'It's not that easy,' she said and I thought she sounded very sad. 'I've sort of come to love him. But he does scare me sometimes. There was a time when I could have had a choice, but not any more. I think I'm stuck with my spirit as long as I live and maybe even longer.'

" 'I'm starting to feel like I'm part of a movie or a weird novel,' I told Josie, 'I'm beginning to wonder just what is real.'

" 'What's real to me may not be real to you,' Josie said. 'I think reality is very relative.'

" 'I don't know what you mean.'

" 'Well, to a large extent our reality is limited by what we believe,' Josie told me. 'Here in this part of Mexico, especially among the Indians, they believe in all sorts of spirits and possession, and since they all believe in it, it is possible. It is real.

" 'They open themselves to all the spirits, the good ones and the bad ones. It gives them magic powers. But it also makes it easier for the bad spirits to hurt them.

" 'Back home, we don't believe in spirits and that's why they hardly ever bother us or help us. Do you understand what I mean?'

" I wasn't sure I understood what Josie was saying because I was no longer sure what I believed. I'd seen so many inexplicable things happen. I really wanted to go home. I was convinced that once I got home this would all seem like a dream and reality would once more become the safe world I had known. But I couldn't leave Josie.

"My beliefs became even more strained. I began to see monsters everywhere, dogs that turned into gods and then back into dogs, giant spiders that started out the size of my fist and right before my eyes grew to be as large as I was and then disappeared. Hairs would turn into snakes and crawl away.

"People would turn into animals, gods, devils, and then back into people. The mountains would suddenly grow huge menacing faces. The skies would open up and I would be exposed to headless bodies, bleeding torsos, gaping ounds, holding their bloody heads in their laps, moaning and rocking with pain.

"I knew I had to go home, but I was afraid to go alone now. I began to feel as though any physical action could mean I had killed someone. If I ate a plate of rice at the wrong time, I'd feel I was eating someone's heart. Food would stick in my mouth. After awhile I just stopped eating.

"At night I'd feel my tiny bedroom was a tomb that I had to escape from. But where could I go? I couldn't sleep any more. I was getting thin, pale, dizzy, and very nervous. I had a hard time catching my breath and my mind seemed to be spinning like a top. At times I felt I'd just like to die, any death that didn't seem too menacing.

"I felt like I was walking a tight rope over a monstrous cavern that included every hell man had ever envisioned, a zombieland where the living dead carry on their eternal search for peace. Hades where spring never comes to bring joy and new life, graves where dead men lay, conscious of their own decaying and of the beauty that could have been their life if only they had accepted it. Greek and Latin hells where people are turned into stones, trees, etc., which stand forever, conscious of their loss, a mental state of loss, regret, deep despair, the knowledge that everything beautiful was once within arm's reach and is now forever gone. A physical hell where living bodies burn, freeze, are cut into bits, stabbed with knives, twisted and torn, dipped in boiling oils, dismembered slowly and painfully and eternally.

"I told Josie, 'We think too much. We feel too much. We hate too much. We hurt too much.'

"Josie and Harik started to worry about me. They saw me as possessed in a different, more dangerous way than Josie was, for Josie had worked out an understanding with her demons. She recognized them, knew their needs, what they wanted, how to satisfy them and how to live with them. But I didn't even realize what was happening to me.

"The chief suggested I go to a priest who could help me. 'It's a regular ceremony for any one who's possessed,' he explained. 'They will either get rid of the spirits that are bothering you or teach you how to get along with them. But we've got to go right away. The longer we wait, the harder it will be.'

"I didn't want to go. But each day I felt worse, more frightened and more lost. My chest felt like I'd swallowed a heavy stone. I wanted to stand on top of the highest mountain in Mexico and shout 'Socorro! Help! Help!' with all the pain and despair in my soul.

"I wafted one person to make me feel I really mattered. I was afraid of Josie, felt Josie was a stranger. And the chief seemed even more foreign than the first day we met, but I needed someone to help me.

"They seemed to be the only ones who cared about me, so I decided to follow their advice. No matter what happened, I knew I couldn't feel any worse than I did right then. My heart was beating like a hammer in the hand of a nervous man who has to finish his work before he can go home. I had to make it slow down so I could get some rest. I had never felt so tired in my life, nor so terrified.

" 'The priest will help you,' Josie promised.

"We all dressed up in our best going-away-from-the-village clothes. The chief got out his old jeep and started getting it into road order. Josie prepared some food for the journey. The chief said it was an all-day affair. The trip itself would take several hours and we wouldn't return home until late.

"The purifying ceremony took place at a shrine to the Virgin Mary. There was a long walk up a mountain to a huge waterfall where the services were held.

"A short, dark priest in a white robe held a heavy silver cross, almost as large as he was. The people who were possessed, mostly women of all sizes and ages, gathered for his blessing. He put the heavy silver Cross to our heads, our chest, our backs as we stood directly under the falling water. He went to each person, one at a time, and with each he would ask as he held the Cross to the person, 'How many are you?'

"The women would answer in strange, faraway voices, giving the number of demons, their names, and other information demanded by the priest.

"When he came to me, I was astonished when a voice came from my mouth saying, 'We are ten.'

" 'What are your names?' the priest asked.

" 'That gruff voice from my throat began listing ten Indian names, none of them familiar to me.

" 'What do you want with her?' the priest asked.

" 'We love her. We want to use her. She gives us a good home.'

" 'Would you leave her?'

" 'No.'

"Then, when my demons refused to leave, the priests and his assistants took whips and wood and beat me and all the other women until we passed out or our devils agreed to depart.

"I passed out. When I came too, I felt better. My intestines felt untied. The rock had stopped beating at my lungs. The band had ceased playing in my head. At last I would be able to rest.

"But by the time we got back to the village, my devils had returned in full force. I felt myself oozing into that cocoon that kept me a prisoner in hell, where every decision meant a test with some significance which escaped me and yet which I felt would decide my fate and that of those I loved.

"That night, there was an awful storm. The wind dashed against the abode hut, shaking it until it seemed as though it might pull it out of the ground and turn it on its side.

"I woke up and heard Josie fighting her devil in the next room. This time I made no effort to help her, since my own devils were attacking me. There was a horror movie going on in my head, a sort of science-fiction theme where everything was possible and only terror was probable.

"I kept seeing monsters in the dark. I lit the candle, thinking the light would scare them away. But the light only emphasized them, making them appear larger and more threatening. I screamed and the chief came to see me.

"I ran to him and gasped out how the creatures from hell were after me. He put his arms around me and tried to quiet me. I relaxed for a moment, then screamed as I saw a horrible shape forming on the ceiling.

"The chief told me to lie still and he'd fix me some tea to quiet my nerves. 'I'm afraid to be alone,' I told him. So he helped me into my robe, and the two of us held hands as we walked in candlelight through the hut into the tiny kitchen.

"The tea put me to sleep.

"The next morning, Josie told me, 'Harik went to town to send a cable to your parents. We talked it over and decided you have to go.'

" 'I don't want to leave you,' I told Josie.

" 'I don't want you to go,' Josie said, 'I'd give anything to keep you here with me. But last night I learned what's happening to you.'

" 'What is happening to me?' I asked.

" 'My devil has fallen in love with you,' Josie said seriously. 'He told me last night. I begged him to leave you alone. I offered him anything he wanted. But he said he must have you.'

" 'So you've got to get away from here. I love you too, and I want you with me. You know that. But I can't let my devil destroy you. You've got to get away before it's too late.'

" 'But what about you?' I asked.

" 'It's too late for me,' Josie said, as though she were pronouncing her own death warrant. 'I can't leave here. My devil won't let me.'

" 'But what will you do when I'm gone?'

" 'I'll still have Harik. He loves me and he knows how to treat my devil. He'll watch over me.'

" 'I can't leave you,' I said.

" 'You must,' Josie told me. She put her arms around me, and we cried for all the pain we had shared and the pain that we'd now go through alone.

"Two days later, my parents arrived. They took a room at the little *pension,* the only thing resembling a hotel in the Mexican village a few miles from the Indian settlement, which was actually a collection of adobe huts, not even enough to house the Indian population so that there were sometimes two or even three generations living in two rooms.

"Mom and Daddy hired a taxi to take them to the Mexican village. They had a hard time hiding their shock at finding Josie and me in such a place and in such a condition.

"I was surprised at how relieved I was to see them. I ran into their arms, cried on their shoulders. It was as if they were angels who had come down to hell to rescue me.

"I really did want to go home.

"Mom helped me pack my bag. At first I tried to choose what to take and what to leave. But once more each decision seemed to carry hidden strings which would determine the fate of the world. So in the end Mom did all the deciding and all the packing.

" 'Aren't you packing your bags, Josie?' Mom asked.

" 'I'm not going,' Josie said, 'I'm married to Harik. I'm his wife and I don't want to leave him.'

" 'But after all of this, surely you want to see your mother,' Mom said. 'The two of us have been out of our minds with worry over you girls. We love you so much. We couldn't believe that you'd really gone. I promised your mother I'd bring you back.'

" 'You must come,' Daddy told Josie. 'We aren't leaving here without you. Come and see your mother and then if you decide you want to come back here, I'm sure you can work something out.'

" 'I can't go,' Josie said, her eyes reflecting the terror she felt.

"When Josie kept refusing to leave, Daddy got very angry. 'If you won't come peacefully, I'll get the Mexican police to help me.I refuse to leave you down here. We told your mother we were bringing you back and we are.'

"Josie saw that she had lost. 'Okay,' she said quietly. 'I'll have a cup of tea, then pack my bags.'

"The chief put his arms around her, and walked her into the little kitchen. 'It'll be good for you to see your mother,' they could hear him telling Josie. 'And you can always come back. I'll be here.' Harik left Josie in the kitchen and returned to the living room, where Mom and Daddy and I were waiting.

"It was an uneasy moment as the chief tried to entertain my parents, who only knew a few words of Spanish. His knowledge of English was almost as limited.

"I was doing a wild dance around the living room. I can't remember why, except maybe it was a farewell dance. I was watching my hands turn into beautiful wild birds which seemed to be flying away from my body. I was twirling and spinning. Mom and Daddy sat there on the homemade sofa, stiffly staring at me, the little girl who was supposed to be their daughter but didn't seem to have much in common with the little girl who had run away.

"From the kitchen there came screams of terror, loud angry shouts, 'I don't want to go! I have to! You must let me alone! I've got to. I won't! I can't! You mustn't make me!' First in English, then in the Indian dialect which Josie used more often now.

"We ran into the kitchen. Josie was sitting quietly on the little wooden chair sipping her tea. She looked up at us and smiled. She took the last gulp and slowly slipped from the chair, to the floor unconscious.

"The chief carried her into the bedroom and lay her on the bed. Daddy wanted to call a doctor, but Harik felt Josie's pulse, put his head to her chest, and said, 'Too late,' one of the few phrases he knew in English. 'Too late.' He shook his head and kept repeating the phrase over and over.

"Mom and Dad went to the Mexican village and got an undertaker and made the necessary arrangements to have Josie's body shipped back to Philadelphia for the funeral. Then we all three flew back home."

"Josie's death, and the circumstances surrounding it, were the most awesome experience of my life. It made me aware, though my upbringing and education made me resist the awareness, that there are spirits, supernatural beings, who not only exist but have the power to control our lives, even kill us, once we enter into relationship with them. I believe that those beings of the netherworld can also be controlled by us for our benefit, if we open ourselves to them and allow them to put us in more profound touch with the universe. That is the purpose of my trip. I want to know more about what happened to me and to Josie back then. I need to come to terms with it, whatever that may mean. I feel somewhat armed, with my knowledge of anthropological methods and the fact that I'm several years older and presumably more mature, but ultimately the results of my quest depend on what kind of person I am."

9
Michelle

Michelle did not become a bona-fide runaway until she was twelve. But she had been building up to it for sometime. When I first met her, she was a small, scrawny eight-year-old. Her large blue eyes were the most arresting feature in her pinched little face. She would come to the park and ask one of the young mothers seated on the benches near the sandbox for ice cream. She would also offer to baby-sit while the women went shopping. Someone always responded to Michelle's plea for ice cream, but as far as I know no one took her up on her offer to baby-sit. In general, the mothers were sympathetic to Michelle and angry at her parents, whoever they were, for their blatant neglect of her. Michelle said that her father was an artist and that her mother worked all day.

Besides panhandling ice cream, Michelle used to hang out at a real-estate office in the neighborhood and get coffee and sandwiches for the brokers and secretaries in return for tips. Michelle was illiterate and did not spend much time in school. The school kept telling her she was a failure so why should she hang around?

Over the years, I ran into Michelle from time to time. She was always optimistic. By the age of twelve she was making money baby-sitting for working mothers. She was rarely in her parent' home, and they did not seem to care. She accepted her parents' neglect, even when it meant being sent to reform school for no other reason than that she was a minor out late at night who did not have parents or substitutes who would come to court for her. She had adult responsibilities, but was punished by the state for demanding adult privileges such as the freedom to be where she liked when she liked.

She solved the after-hours problem, at least temporarily, by becoming a live-in baby-sitter for a young couple with two pre-school children. I would see her in Tompkins Square Park with the two babies in tow. Unlike so many kids who are neglected, she did not become hardened or embittered. Rather she took a caring, nurturing attitude toward others.

In the winter of '67, when Michelle was about sixteen, I ran into her in the Deja Vu, an eatery across from the park that specialized in hot and iced cider. She was with two runaways, whose fathers were in the military. Both girls were voluble, full of their recent adventures and misadventures. Both were grateful to Michelle for having found them a place to crash and part-time jobs at the Deja Vu while they got themselves together enough so they could decide what to do next They were convinced that their straight-laced parents wouldn't just say, 'Oh, I see, they've run away," and leave it at that. They were sure they'd be discovered in New York and were planning to move to a rural commune as soon as possible. Michelle said she'd help them find a ride as soon as they decided where they wanted to go.

The next time I saw Michelle she was participating in a spontaneous demonstration on Second Avenue near St. Mark's Place.

Many of the runaways in the East Village became involved in the political scene in the late sixties, a political scene that consisted largely of demonstrations and was characterized, above all, by exuberance. It was natural for the runaway to take part in these demonstrations; he was likely to be hanging out in the places where they occurred. Further, the demonstrations in one way or another were all protests against the injustice, immorality, and screwed-up values the runaway, as a fugitive on the fringes of society, was more aware of on a gut level than most people.

Many demonstrations occurred spontaneously, the result of hot weather and no money to go anywhere. The demonstration I saw Michelle in was like that. It was on Second Avenue, one of the many "the streets belong to the people" demonstrations that took place in '67 and '68 and colorful with tambourines and incense, bells and flowers. The participants danced in a circle to the thythms created by the tambourines and their own voices chanting, "The streets belong to the people, the streets belong to the people, the streets belong to the people" and rising to a crescendo. A crowd gathered around them and more dancers and chanters joined the group, all of them young, gorgeously, if raggedly fressed, and intensely appealing.

The police came. It was to be expected. In a sense if was what the dance was about, the fact that those who really own the streets—or rather, their emissaries, the police—won't countenance dancing and singing on them. The excuse is that dancing and singing, except at authorized points and places, will disturb the orderly flow of traffic.

There were other similar demonstrations, except that they were a bit less spontaneous and attended by larger numbers of people. Several hundred people, informed by word of mouth, showed up for the yip-in at Grand Central Station. Michelle's boyfriend, Perry Paranoia, asked Michelle if she wanted to go to the yip-in with him.

"What's a yip-in?" she asked.

"It's a more advanced stage of a be-in," he answered.

Michelle arrived at Perry's house wearing a flowered mini-skirt dress, barefoot sandals, and several bracelets.

"Come in," said Perry, "The door's open." He was lying on his elbows on the bed. Michelle stood there in front of him. "You're so powerful standing there like that," he told her. "Sit down so we can be equals."

She sat on the bed beside him, then turned her body around so her head was on his lap. She looked up at him, smiling.

"We have about an hour and a half before we should leave. Let's smoke some grass," he said.

They smoked a joint he'd rolled before on banana papers.

"You finish it," he said. I'm pretty stoned already."

"Why is this thing going to happen at Grand Central Station?" she asked. "I mean, it's so vast and impersonal."

"We're going to make it smaller and more personal."

Michelle sat up and hugged Perry.

"Can I brush your hair?" he asked.

"Sure," she replied.

He brushed her hair from side to side, under and over, and then began to tease it. When he was finished it stood out several inches from her head on both sides, much more bouffant than she would have thought it could look without a set.

"Your hair looks different, too," Michelle remarked.

"I set it with curlers," he replied.

Michelle laughed. "Seems weird for a guy," she said, "but, I guess there's no reason you shouldn't. It looks good."

"Now you skin looks too pale. Not too pale," Perry amended, "just pale. Would you like to see how you'd look with darker skin?"

"Sure," she said. "How're you going to accomplish that?"

He pressed something out of a tube and began to smooth it over Michelle's face and neck. The effect was gorgeous. The artifically tan skin made her blue eyes incredibly brillant.

Perry took six joints out of the top drawer of his green dresser. He put five into a package of cigarettes, which he put into his shirt pocket, and lit the sixth. It was almost time to go.

The central area of Grand Central Station was a mob scene in slow motion thronged with people, two or three thousand of them, with eyes wide open, that said, "Take me, I'm yours"; passing joints, waving incense or just waving. Figures in flowing garments, tattered raiment, bright patches of color more frequent than in your average crowd. Faces were radiant with coming-together. Two of them climbed up the clock high above the crowd in order to stop time, and a cheer reverberated through the hall in praise of their accomplishment.

Then the cops appeared. Swinging clubs as mercilessly as they moved, they pushed through the crowd. Michelle could see the flow of those demonstrators caught between the cops and the rest of the people in the station. Then the whole crowd began to move toward the exits, an exodus that speeded up very gradually, yet unmistakably, in the wake of the cops. No one was going to be trampled, crashed.

Despite the density of the crowd, Michelle felt relieved, even elated. Then, without warning, she was brought back to earth with a thud when a few feet away a man's skull was cracked open.

"Perry," she said. "Did you see that?"

"Yeah," he replied. "Don't panic. It won't help. We'll be at the exit soon."

Cops flanked all of the walls up to the exit. They lined the streets outside. Michelle and Perry walked quickly, a step behind the people in front of them, a step in front of the people in back. Finally, they were outside in the balmy spring air of the city. Other people were trying to get out but some, it seemed, were trying to get back in. Most of the kids, were waiting around, waiting to see what would happen next. Michelle watched as four badly hurt people were led out of the station by their friends.

The yip-in ended up in Central Park, where the crowd made fires to keep warm, which the police put out almost as fast as they could get them going. They stayed to see the sun come up. At least that was the explanation most of them gave to representatives of the news media who appeared on the scene. They outlasted the night. Then they began to ebb away, two, three, four at a time. The police, satisfied that they were too tired to make further claims on public property at that point, began to thin out in number, too.

Michelle and Perry went back to Perry's house and the two spent most of the day sleeping in each other's arms.

That summer of '68 will probably be best remembered for the Democratic convention in Chicago and the demonstrations that took place in response to the travesty of democracy it became.

The race was between Hubert Humphrey, popularly known as a political whore/hack, who had long since sold out anything resembling humanitarian ideals and Eugene McCarthy, "clean Gene," whose main attraction to those who supported him was that he promised to end the war in Vietnam "immediately" if elected.

The war was condemned widely for its illegality and immorality. The U.S.A. had, because of its continuation of the war, become a bully in the eyes of the world, as well as to vast numbers of its own citizens. And since everyone knew that the Republicans would nominate a hawk, the Dbmocratic convention appeared to be a showdown between the nation's lust for power and its conscience.

Michelle went to the Chicago demonstration in a red truck belonging to someone named Sam along with four other young people. One of them, Laurie, was a runaway and two, Billy Boy and Hammerhead, were draft-dodgers.

They left New York about a week before the demonstrations were to take place so that they could take a leisurely drive across the eastern third of the country. They'd thought of psychedelicizing the truck, but considered their youth, long hair, and the like, and decided they'd probably have enough trouble with a plain red truck.

Michelle knew Murdock better than any of the others. She had met him in a friend's store, a thrift shop on Fourth Street. He had burst through the door, saying, "Hey, man, what's happening?" Liz, the woman who owned the store, had replied, "Right now we're folding these clothes that someone donated last night."

"Far out," Murdock had replied. "Far fucking out."

Liz asked Murdock what he was into.

"Hey, man," he said. "There'x going to be this huge fucking gathering in Chicago during the Democratic convention. We're going to have our convention. Hah. Those people will fucking slip out."

"Won't they be expecting some sort of demonstration?" asked Michelle.

"Yeah, but not the kind of demonstration they're going to get. It's going to be fucking mannouth."

"Hey," he said, making sure that he still held their attention, "did you people hear what's been going down at Columbia? It was fucking beautiful. The way those kids took over the buildings. I was there, man. You wouldn:t believe what happened. Fucking incredible. We weren't taking any shit. The administration had to call the pigs to get us out; had to come out and show whose side they're really on. Couldn't hide behind their liberal bullshit this time.

"There's gonna be some newsreel flicks ˑshown in Tompkins Square tonight," he continued. "Films from Cuba and the Belgian Congo, very far-out stuff."

Might be good to see some flicks in the park tonight," said Michelle, turning to Liz.

"You really ought to check it out, man," said Murdock on his way out.

Murdock was a revolutionary whirlwind whose methods were confrontation with the cops, ripping-off the system, and "bring your own media." Too frenetic even to smoke much grass, though he talked about it, Murdock didn't need any chemical turn-on; he was high on the revolution, revolving round and round with amazing speed.

Murdock's friend Sam, who owned the red truck and at times seemed to be owned by it, shated most of his beliefs but in almost all instances was a lot more cynical about what was happening and what probably would develop. Sam had spent a couple of years in jail for refusing to be inducted into the Army and was now out on parole. When he'd gone to jail, he'd assumed that sweeping political changes were close at hand and that resisting the draft would bring those changes closer. He wasn't at all sure now if any political activity that he or any of his peers had engaged in would do more than make headlines. He now felt it would have been smarter to simply evade the draft, like Hammerhead and Billy boy.

Laurie, the runaway, was a light-skinned black girl with a pretty, almost kewpie-doll face. She was the oldest child in a large family. Her father had left home when she was sixteen and she had been left with the responsibility for caring for her younger siblings. Since her mother worked and was too ill most of the time to both work and assume household chores, there was only Laurie. She had left her mother's home upstate and come to the city to live with her grandmother because the load was too heavy for her to bear. She sympathized with her mother, but resented having to raise five kids that she hadn't brought into the world. She swore she'd never have any kids of her own. Laurie lived with Hammerhead. They played house in a three-room apartment on Tenth Street, vying with each other over who would be the baby.

Hammerhead was an outrageous hedonist, rip-roaring nihilist, up-front masochist. He looked great even with a three-day shadow. He dressed in basic black polo and chinos and had a cloyingly boyish grin. He teased Laurie a lot in a flattering sort of way. She giggled a lot and nagged him and flirted with him in the same breath.

Billy Boy was a tall lanky southerner with shoulder-length blond hair. He was silent most of the time, and when he did speak, it usually put people a little off balance, since they hadn't been let in on the drift of his thoughts.

So the six of them set out in the red truck. They stopped for gas at a garage on Second Street, where Murdock gave a joint and a copy of an underground paper to the astonished gas-station attendant. They started off in high spirits. It was good to be on the road. It was going to be an adventure.

They made several stops in small towns, where they attracted a lot of attention because of their long hair, bare feet, and the like. This gave them an opportunity to rap with people about where they were going and why. Murdock did more rapping than anyone else. They also distributed underground papers; Murdock would hand one of the papers to an incredulous middle-aged matron¢telling her with an unmistakable sincerity that prevented her from resisting him¢that the regular papers lied.

Government and big business controlled not only the wealth of the country, but the people's minds because they owned the media that feeds most of us our information. "You ought to at least give another point of view a chance to influence you," he'd say.

Michelle listened to Murdock, and after awhile she began to get the hang of it. By the time they got to Cleveland, where they remained for a couple of days, she wasn't too shy to begin talking to a group of students sitting on the grass in a park near Western Reserve.

They were staying with some people who ran an underground paper. There seemed to be more space in Cleveland than in New York, Michelle thought. There was plenty of room for the six of them, in addition to the two people who usually stayed in the apartment. Sam had arranged for them to stay there.

He and Murdock had also brought along some newsreel films and a projector and screen, and they thought that they street they were staying on would be perfect for showing films. It was a dead-end street near Western Reserve and there were a lot of people outside in the early evening.

In order to attract a crowd before showing the films, and because they felt like it, they took a bunch of kitchen utensils to use as percussion instruments and dance to. They wore kerchiefs, jewelry, anything they could grab that was gaudy. They began marching down the street in single file, banging wooden spoons against pots. Michelle carried a maracas she had made from a coffee can and some dried beans. They played follow the leader, taking turns leading and following. Finally, they danced in a circle, not all of them doing the same thing but rather movements that were complimentary. They discarded their instruments and chanted, meanwhile doing a snail. When at last they were wound up tight, their voices rising to a crescendo, their energy broke and they stood silently.

Michelle was stunned by the volume of the applause that greeted them. They had collected quite a crowd, a crowd that took them in, during the movie and after. They felt as if they had lived there forever; it was hard to believe that they had just arrived that day, and would leave to continue on their journey tomorrow.

That night Sam, Murdock, Billy Boy, and Laurie fell asleep exhausted. Michelle and Hammerhead were tired but too excited to sleep without thinking about what had happened and what was likely to come. Naturally, they decided to do their reflecting with each other, and one of the things reflected in their eyes and voices was their lust for each other.

Earlier that day they had been sitting in the back of the truck along with Laurie and Billy Boy (Sam and Murdock were in front). Laurie's head was resting on Hammerhead's lap, while he and Michelle stared at each other silently. He had given her an orgasm with his big toe and they had both felt perverse and groovy, Hammerhead because it was literally behind Laurie's back. She was awake and could have turned around at any moment.

Michelle had enjoyed Billy Boy looking on with a sober "what have we here" expression on his lean, handsome face. His cavernous blue eyes gave little away, so she was free to imagine what he might be thinking, to create her audience, as it were.

Now Michelle and Hammerhead had a full double bed to perform on. They could take off their clothes, make love sounds; they were free to do as they liked. The big mirror across the room enticed them even more. They could now be their own and each other's audience and have each other at the same time¢or could they? They undressed before the mirror and began to touch each other's bodies lightly.

Hammerhead told Michelle about the time his mother had been driving him somewhere or other. "Then she stopped the car in this secluded place, surrounded by trees. She began to kiss me and fondle me. Well, she wanted to make it with me, I swear."

"How old were you ethen?" asked Michelle, assuming it was a childhood fantasy that had become more spectacular as time passed.

"It was last year," he replied. "I was nineteen."

Michelle laughed, not knowing whether to believe him or not.

"Hey," she said, "I don't want to be your mother."

Hammerhead made a mock-tearful face.

"Who will you be then?" he asked.

"I'll be your sister, if you like," Michelle answered.

"I think I could dig that," he said decisively. "I've never had a sister."

Their love-making didn't live up to their expectations. Somehow everything seemed to flatten out once they turned away from the mirror. It was as if it contained the real world, and that what they usually thought of as real was two-dimensional. They drank up a bottle of beer that they found in the refrigerator, and laughed about inadequacy in general, which seemed to make more sense than crying about it. They fell asleep effortlessly and separately; Hammerhead didn't want Laurie to know about his escapade with Michelle, and she in her turn was considered by Murdock and the group to be his girl.

By the time the six got to Chicago, they were exhausted and grimy. It seemed like a perfect stroke of luck when Sam and Murdock returned to the truck from the MOB office that was coordinating the demonstrations and said that they had a place to stay. It sounded like a gas.

"It's these people who used to be communists and became capitalists and made a lot of money in TV's and stereos and shit," said Murdock. They have this big fancy house, and I think they have a teen-aged daughter. Anyhow, they're letting us crash there along with a McCarthy delegate and his son from New York."

A chorus of "far outs" greeted Murdock's news.

The place turned out to be practically a mansion. It had three floors and an attic. Just three people lived there Mommy, Daddy, and daughter Wendy. There was a son, but he had moved away.

They had come just in time to watch the first day of the convention on an enormous color TV. Michelle thought color TV made everything seem like fun, like a puppet show. They took time out for a sumptuous meal of leftovers and again tried to make sense out of what was happening on the screen. It seemed to Michelle that more delegates seemed to be for McCarthy, but maybe that was just wishful thinking.

They were to sleep in the attic, along with Wendy and Jon, the fourteen-year-old son of the New York delegate. They also had the use of one of the downstairs rooms. Laurie and Murdock decided to sleep there, since it looked like a long rap session was just getting under way in the attic and they wanted some rest.

Wendy went into the storage part of the attic and came out wearing a Garbo hat. She had evidently also fetched something else, because after everyone had admired the effect of the hat she asked them conspiratorially if they'd like to smoke some grass. It was fine smoke, and soon all of them were stoned, including fourteen-year-old Jon, who'd never smoked before.

"What do you do besides model period hats," said Sam to Wendy.

"Go to school," she answered. I go to the University of Chicago."

"Is it fun?" he asked.

"Mostly it's a bore, but there's one course I really dig. It's a lit course. I got into reading J.D. Salinger and ended up reading everything he wrote. Then I did a paper on the works and sent him a copy. He sent back a really cool letter."

"Which story is your favorite?" asked Sam.

"*Bananafish,*" Wendy answered. It's so tragic, when Seymour dies. It made me shiver all over.

"My favorite is still *Catcher in the Rye.* I always identified with Holden, exploring, taking it all in, giving each person and scene its due. Kind of cool and sympathetic at the same time.

"I dug *Catcher in the Rye,* too, but for a different reason. I liked the idea that Holden wanted to save the children from falling off the precipice of their wonderland into pain and mistrust, and, you know, not being able to love themselves and other people. Maybe, that's what this whole demonstration thing is about. That's why McCarthy has to win. He's trying to be a grown-up Holden Caulfield. Hoping he'll get a chance to improve things a little so it won't be the same nightmare for the next generation."

"Even if you're right that McCarthy has a burning desire to make the world safe for the kiddies, I don't see how that makes it inevitable that he'll win either the nomination or the election. But, it's a beautiful thought, and"

He caught his breath as their eyes met. "I'd like to make love with you," he said.

They made love, with Wendy on top, while the rest looked on. Hammerhead was open-mouthed, astonished at first. His expression metamorphosed into a sideways grin. Wendy was in ecstacy, flying free.

They spent most of the next day riding from place to place in the truck. Michelle wanted to go to the demonstration in Lincoln Park but she didn't want to go alone, so she remained with the group in the truck. In the evening they all went to an auditorium, and listened intently to the speeches and music. They were packed into the auditorium, three thousand of them.

"And now introducing the stars of our revolution," Michelle thought. Norman Mailer mostly said he couldn't stay because he had to go home to finish an article. Genet looked older than the world. No, he looked ageless. His accent at first had the effect of making his words seem garbled to Michelle. Something about police dogs. Then she understood. He said that what they were about to encounter in the way of police brutality, no matter how outrageous it might seem, would be no more than a taste, a faint whiff of what black people had been suffering in America these four hundred years.

William Burroughs spoke, Allan Ginsburg chanted, Ian and Sylvia sang tunefully, a band played raucously. Then someone announced the showing of a six-reel film. It was strange. Most people wanted to leave at that point, to get out into the fray or whatever, but they remained out of consideration for the film maker.

Then they were out on Michigan Avenue. Soon after they had arrived, there was a "changing of the guard." The cops gave way to the National Guard. A lot of people cheered, feeling that the National Guard was likely to be a mixed bag; that there was a possibility of communication with some of them. The crowds weaved in and out. Michelle and Laurie stuck together, but got separated from the men.

They exchanged wary glances. Their relationship had been more competitive than cooperative from the start. Each always tried to best the other in conversation. Michelle had felt that Laurie was a conversational leach. It seemed that every time Michelle recounted an experience, Laurie would mention a similar experience that in some way was a little more far-out. Then Michelle realized that she had done the same thing. She felt sad about it and wished they could be friends, but she didn?t know how to begin. And here they were, at it again, trying to outdo each other in flirting with the soldiers, getting them to drop their guard. Neither was very successful.

Finally, they ran into Sam, who told them they?d been kicked out of the place they?d stayed the night before for giving pot to their sixteen-year-old daughter.

"What?" exclaimed Michelle.

"I decided she has to live there. Why fuck things up for her? And I found us another place. It's in the basement of a church. We'll get a chance to use our sleeping bags."

They parked a few doors down from the church, which was in a Puerto Rican section of the city. Michelle stayed in the truck to change her clothes and the others went to the church. When she got out of the truck, Michelle saw that two buildings connected with the church. When she knocked on the door of one—which turned out to be the wrong one—she got no response and knocked again. Meanwhile, a police car had stopped in front of the church. One of the cops got out to investigate.

"What are you doing here?" he asked Michelle.

"My friends are inside the church, and I'm supposed to join them," she replied.

The cop just stood there menacingly. "I guess I'll have to take you in," he said.

Fortunately, at that moment Sam came through the side door of the other building and said, "We were wondering what happened to you." Michelle had never been so glad to see anyone.

"If I see you walking around this neighborhood," the cop said to Michelle, almost casually, "I'll kill you."

"Welcome to Chicago," she thought.

Scheduled for the next afternoon was the big demonstration in the park on Michigan Avenue, across the street from the big hotels at which most of the delegates were staying. It was a sunny August day, and ice-cream and soda carts were doing a booming business. Michelle was alone, because she had felt too restless to wait for the others to come to the park. A stage had been set up and several people had already made speeches.

Michelle wasn't into listening to speeches; she was into the ebb and flow of the crowds. On the one hand, it was like any sunny Sunday mob scene in the park, and on the other, it was a demonstration; a political happening that would, ironically, be complete only with the acknowledgment of the enemy, which was both dreaded and desired by the demonstrators.

The police began to mass near the stage. A group of people who seemed to have rehearsed the occasion began to link arms, several feet from the stage, and asked that the demonstrators either join in the chain or get behind it.

Michelle was ready this time. It was just like the yip-in. The cops charged suddenly, without warning, swinging their clubs as they moved forward. This time, Michelle was closer to the action. She heard screams and moans, saw blood and fallen bodies, quite close by. It was just luck that she wasn't hit.

The crowd in the park headed for the exits on Michigan Avenue, where they were greeted by the mule train representing the slain Martin Luther King. All of a sudden there were thousands of people in the street. The mood, despite the recent brush with the cops, was one of celebration. It would not last long. Again the police massed into phalanxes and drove the Michigan Avenue demonstrators up the side streets.

Michelle, who had slithered through the crowd when the cops charged as if she were riding the New York subways, found herself part of a fairly well-defined group of ten, a gang looking for direction.

"Let's trash," she commanded playfully. They ran down the street knocking over garbage cans until the momentum of the group ebbed.

"Let's liberate the street," she yelled.

They were on the cross street when the conical police bull horns sounded. Michelle was intently at work on her self-assigned task. When she looked up, it was just in time to move out of the way of a police car coming toward her at seventy miles an hour. She had seen the glint in the driver's eye. He wouldn't have stopped.

To her surprise, Michelle found herself alone. Where had the others disappeared to?

She wanted to get back to Michigan Avenue and was heading in that direction when she saw two cops heading toward her, clubs raised. She about-faced quickly and ran. A plainclothes-man, conversing with a crony outside a bar attempted to trip her, but she saw his foot in time and deftly skirted it. She ran three more blocks before she dared to turn around.

Michelle saw the mule train coming around the bend and decided to latch onto the procession that followed it slowly, two by two, down sleazy, broken-down Madison Street between the endless pairs of wary dark eyes, neither encouraging nor rejecting the marchers, that showed from the rundown porches, hopelessly cracked windows, and scarred ads on desolate walls.

At the end of this street, near the bus depot, stood the SDA office. Here the march ended. At last Michelle was reunited with Murdock, Sam, Laurie, and Hammerhead, who were watching the events they had just lived through on a beat-up black-and-white TV. Murdock was cheering the tiny figures on the screen as they played their parts a second time on video tape.

"Where's Billy Boy?" Michelle asked Sam.

"We don't know. We're worried about him. I mean, a lot of people have been more or less badly injured."

They drove around in the truck, trying to find Billy Boy, and finally found him walking down the street alone. They stopped and honked. He looked up, grinned, and pulled himself aboard.

"What happened?" exclaimed Laurie, noting the bandage that covered the right side of his forehead.

"I got hit. Some damned pig."

"Does it hurt?" she asked.

"Yeah, it kind of comes in waves. But it won't get infected." One of the medics at the demonstration washed it with an antiseptic."

Billy Boy winced at intervals. They had the feeling he was being stoical.

As they drove along, Billy Boy had the idea they should collect rocks to throw at the windows of the big department stores in the loop. Murdock informed the group that a man had just been shot down by the cops for doing exactly that so the idea was vetoed.

The next day's demonstration, which was referred to as the Dick Gregory March because he led it and said—for the benefit of the press—that he was inviting everyone (several thousand demonstrators) to his house for a beer, began in the early afternoon.

On the evening before, what had posed as a democratic political process in the U.S.A. seemed to come to an end when several McCarthy delegates were bodily removed from the convention floor to prevent them from casting their votes. "Is this the beginning of an up-front police state?" everyone wondered. Several of the delegates were at the Dick Gregory demonstration which, despite what had happened at the convention the evening before, gave many demonstrators a feeling of security. "Surely the police wouldn't riot again with so many VIPs present," was the line of reasoning.

As it turned out, the delegates were prime targets for arrest, and police tactics switched from billy clubs to tear gas.

Michelle, who was near the front of the procession, received more than a healthy sahre of tear gas when a canister exploded a few feet away.

Again her long-time residence in New York stood her in good stead. She discovered that for her at least, the tear gas, while certainly unpleasant, was not really incapacitating.

Michelle left Chicago the next day, along with Sam, Murdock, Laurie, Hammerhead, and Billy Boy, in the red truck. Sam planned to go to Michigan, so the others would have to find other rides back to New York.

"I'm not in a big hurry," Sam told them. "I plan to stop at this farm near Chicago. There's going to be a national SDS meeting there, and I thought I'd check it out. You can all come if you like.

They went with Sam, figuring that they'd find rides from there.

The meeting was in progress when they arrived. It was being held in the living room of the larger of the two houses on the farm. The discussion, which mostly involved people from different parts of the country, especially the Midwest, seemed aimed at attacking people from New York for assuming that they were SDS.

Michelle was bored. She went outside, where she spotted three horses inside a corral. She climbed up on the fence, and a da ed mare came over to her. There weren't any saddles, and she'd never ridden a horse before. After falling off three times, she decided to give up for the time being.

Michelle entered the maller house, which was about ten yards from the larger one. It was dark inside and at first it seemed that no one was there. Shen she climbed the stairs, however, she heard a man's voice call, "Michelle, come over here." She faced the corner from which the voice had come and saw Sam, there in the gloom. She went over to him and lay down beside him. They began to make love. When Laurie entered the room they were completely undressed.

"Hey, Laurie," Sam yelled, "we're over here."

"We're havingan alternate meeting," Michele added.

Laurie undressed, too, and lay down, propped up on an elbow on the other side of Sam.

Group grope. Michelle and Laurie leaned across Sam, felt each other's breasts, hips, thighs, excited yet feeling a little strange. Sam wanted to make it with both of them and after awhile it became their goal, too. But Sam felt too pressured by his own desires and those of the girls and couldn't get an erection. Laurie left and somehow Michelle wasn't interested in continuing with Sam once she had gone. It would have been anti-climactic.

Michelle dressed quickly, then satsilently until Sam was ready to leave. They went back to the meeting together. Michelle slept with Murdock that night and Laurie slept with Hammerhead.

The next day the group split up. Sam went to Michigan; Hammerhead and Laurie got a ride with a couple from the Midwest who planned to visit New York for a few weeks; Murdock decided to hang out at the farm for a couple of days; and Michelle and Billy Boy got a ride in a van as riders numbers eight and nine.

Michelle and Billy Boy got to know each other better on the trip back. They could hardly help it, with Michelle sitting on Billy Boy's lap for most of the ride. By the time they reached New York, they had decided that Michelle would move in with Billy Boy.

Michelle was in love. Billy Boy was beautiful, tall and lanky, with a sensitive, bony face, and deep-set, bottomless blue eyes.

Everything he did was somehow right—his poems, the murals he painted on the walls, and most of all, the way he grasped situations, which made each moment full and exciting. And he wasn't so shy now that he was in his own scene. His friends were mostly young, many of them runaways, street people. Billy was twenty. Hammerhead, Murdock, and Sam were older and more experienced than he was, which to some extent had intimidated him. Here and now, he was in his element.

Murdock came over to visit from time to time. The relationship between him and Michelle was awkward. He behaved almost as if she didn't exist. Michelle realized it was because she had hurt his pride. But she felt they should reach some kind of understanding, if he was to continue to visit. But when she tried to approach him in a friendly way, he rebuffed her. She didn't like it, and didn't know what to do about it.

Meanwhile Billy Boy had become progressively more outspoken about his revolutionary commitment. He began to talk about guerrilla warfare, burning, and bombing. Michelle hoped that his frustration would not lead to some ill-conceived action, which would harm him without helping anyone else.

Billy Boy, Murdock, and three or four other men would sit around the kitchen table talking revolution. Michelle felt left out, hurt, and angry. She was equally upset when Billy Boy went to see Lisa. Lisa had lived with him before and moved out, probably for the same reasons that now made Michelle think of leaving. But Michelle had no place to go and besides, when she and Billy Boy were alone together and especially when they were tripping, which they did frequently, she knew that she really didn't want to be anywhere else or with anyone else.

One of Billy Boy's friend, Rick, was older than the others, at least twenty-five. He was extraordinarily polite and accommodating, and in contrast to the others, always seemed to have some bread. Rick seemed to be very impressed with Billy Boy, and agreed with almost everything he said. Rick was especially enthusiastic when Billy Boy talked about guerrilla warfare. Michelle mistrusted Rick but couldn't pin the feeling down. She knew that if she told Billy Boy that she didn't dig his new admirer he would only put her down, so she said nothing.

Billy was the one who conceived the idea of bombing a bank, but it was Rick who insisted on a particular bank. Rick also offered Billy and Murdock an abundance of information about explosives, timing devices, and so forth.

Finally, the day was set. It was to be a midtown bank, and Michelle, who had not been asked to participate in the planning, who had in fact been discouraged from making a contribution throughout the proceedings, was conscripted to be the driver.

Michelle soon found herself in the midst of what she hoped was a nightmare but knew in her heart was stark reality. For the first time in her life she didn't feel that the situation she was in could be reversed. That she and the others had been arrested was bad enough. She had been aware all along of the possibility. What was so unacceptable was that Rick had turned them in. He was an informer, an agent provocateur, and she had sensed it and said nothing. She thought bitterly that Billy or Murdock would not have paid any attention to her suspicions.

Her eyes wandered around the cell. There were about forty women crowded together, most of them prostitutes and about three-quarters of them black. They were mini-skirted, bewigged, and bejewelled as if they contrived for the same garrishly stunning appeal as the neon lights they competed with for the patronage of thrill seekers who paid cash for their kicks.

These were the girls she'd known at reform school. They were as tough and sophisticated as she'd remembered them. They were women now, still brazen and cunning, still enmeshed in a system that hit them again and again, each time faster and harder than even they could hit back. They griped about the cops who'd turned them in, about the Johns who'd tried to take advantage of them and escaped while they, the women, had to pay for their mutual "crime." But basically they accepted the lock-up as an undesirable, but inevitable concomitant of their way of life. On some level they'd been conned into thinking they were criminals.

Between complaints, most of the women seemed to be in high spirits. They exchanged gossip and fashion news with each other and with the matrons.

"How's your friend Clara?" asked a voluptuous woman wearing a form-fitting chartreuse pants-and-sweater outfit.

"She's sick, honey," the other woman, tall and slim and wearing an enormous blond wig, answered, "I went to see her in Bellevue, and they don't even know what's wrong with her."

"Either that or they're just too high and mighty to tell her, said a third woman. "Those doctors are bastards."

What's that lipstick you're wearing?" the woman in the blond wig said to a very young woman in a very short yellow mini-skirt and high black boots.

"Persimmon passion," she replied.

"Well, it certainly suits you," said the woman in the blond wig.

·After awhile most of the women just sat and stared vacantly, waiting. A few went to sleep.

Finally Michelle was let out of the cell and admitted to the courtroom. The arraignment was an even worse bummer than the arrest had been. Michelle had expected to feel a sense of solidarity with Billy Boy, even with Murdock. Instead, she felt completely alone, almost as alienated from them as she was from the judge, the cops, and from Rick, who smirked at them from time to time as he gave his incriminating testimony.

The people she felt closest to were the women she had just been with. She was with them, if she was with anybody.

*   *   *

"I always felt like a mercenary in someone else's war" said Michelle at a women's consciousness-raising meeting. Michelle's words were followed by applause and shouts of approval. She was out on bail, and knowing that her days of freedom were numbered, resolved not to waste them. She had forced herself—against her "natural" inclinations to be timid, to await overtures from others—to call all the women she could think of to this meeting.

She found that she had broken a dam, and unleashed the surging and bottomless fury of the sea.

The first meeting was chaotic with everyone talking at once, telling all the others how she had been mistreated by her father, brother, boss, husband, lover, comrade, in gory and evocative detail. No more secrets. No more pretending that one had always been the chosen, the adored, the beloved. Here and now was a new freedom in this sharing of grievances, grief, and righteous anger—freedom and ecstacy.

By the fourth meeting, Michelle, who had become the leader—because the threat that hung over her, the likelihood that she would be given a long prison sentence, gave her perceptions greater depth and immediacy—decided that it was time for them to make their stand against the oppression of all women public.

"I think that the consciousness-raising sessions that we've had so far have been really productive for all of us, and I think we should continue to have them," said Michelle. "But I don't think we should limit ourselves to consciousness-raising. If we do that, it becomes mere therapy. I think we should plan some public action that relates to the oppression of women. We've got to confront the male Establishment."

"You've spoken a great deal about the oppression of prostitutes. Maybe we should demonstrate in favor of the legalization of prostitution." Sarah was a pale, intense young woman who was having a rough time trying to make it as a singer-composer.

"I don't know about that," said Laurie, who'd just broken up with Hammerhead because he was too drugged out or too inconsiderate (it didn't matter which any more) to visit her when she was sick in the hospital. "The whole direction of radical politics seems to be that you've got to speak out against your own oppression. I mean, I think women who are prostitutes should lead any demonstrations in favor of the legalization of prostitution."

"Besides," added Belinda, who had spent years doing typing and answering telephones for various radical organizations, "prostitutes aren't oppressed only by cops and lawyers and judges. They're oppressed by pimps who exploit them economically and emotionally, and maybe most of all by customers who think of women as pieces of ass, as cesspools, and who think of prostitutes as those things and as circus freaks in addition. I mean, legalization by itself could be completely consistent with a male-chauvinist position."

"I think that makes sense," said Michelle. "I've got another idea. There's going to be a bill before the state legislature for reform of the abortion laws. I think we ought to demonstrate, not for reform, but for repeal."

The women decided that instead of a demonstration they would present a play, a true-to-life drama, the message of which would be the necessity of repealing the abortion laws. As they created the play, each of them became more deeply aware than she had been before that women as a group, as a class, were controlled by men because of their inability to control their own reproductive lives.

They performed the play on a sunny Saturday in May, in front of St. Patrick's Cathedral. Ondine, the actress of the group, who had recently gone through the ordeal of procuring an abortion and had almost died from loss of blood after the operation, was the star of the drama.

Ondine spoke the opening lines, portraying with all the panic of a trapped animal a woman confronted by an unwanted pregnancy. "I'm pregnant," she cried. "Oh, no! What shall I do?" A group of women chant in chorus, "Go to a gynecologist." Belinda, in a lab coat and fake mustache, played the gynecologist, who says he has to examine her first. The chorus huddle around Belinda and Ondine while the examination presumably takes place. Then Belinda pronounces Ondine pregnant, and when she asks for an abortion, says, "That's criminal. How could you think of such a thing? You've had your fun. Now you've got to pay for it." When Ondine asks, "What about the father?" Belinda says, "Yes, you should have thought about the father of your child beforehand."

The pregnant woman appeals to her boyfriend, who accuses her of promiscuity in order to avoid giving her money for an abortion. She is forced to put off the abortion for a month in order to get together the money for it, and dies at the hands of a quack abortionist.

The actresses were assailed by hecklers, mostly women, who called them "whores who sleep with any man on the street" and "murderers," and demanded that they be arrested. Soon the police arrived, threatening to do just that.

But there was a sprinkling of women in the audience who murmured rather than shouted, who expressed such sentiments as "You know, they're right. It's wrong for a woman to have to have a child she doesn't want." "Why should a woman be punished more than a man for something they both did?" "Just because it's always been that way doesn't mean it always has to be that way."

Michelle split just as the police began to close in on the small, but determined group of actresses. I've asked all of our mutual friends and acquaintances if they've seen or heard from her but no one has or will admit to it. It's been four years since Michelle went underground.

Conclusion

The philosophy of today's runaways seems to be that life is too short to waste time where you don't want to be.

The puritanical tradition of deferring pleasure, living for the future at all times, and putting business before pleasure is still very influential in our society. School is a preparation for getting a job so we can earn enough money to save something for our retirement. Some of us waste our entire lives preparing for that great day when we can finally relax and enjoy life.

Like the elderly couple that Bunny and Josie met on their way to Mexico, many people save all their lives for that one trip to Europe, South America, or the Caribbean. Sometimes, when they get there, they are too old and too sick to enjoy it.

Recently, however, our society is showing some rebellion against that old-time principle of living for the future. All the airlines offer "fly now and pay later" plans and more and more Americans are beginning to live on credit in order to get things they would otherwise have to save years for—cars, houses, furniture, etc. This way of life, however, has a way of messing up the future before it arrives.

Nevertheless, most Americans have a hard time adjusting to the present, enjoying it, making the most of it, living each moment as though it were the only one left.

But not the young, who seem to have decided that they won't make the same mistake.

Little Bit once told me, "I want to live one day at a time, one hour at a time, one minute at a time. I want to live each moment to its fullest. If you're sleeping, really sleep. If you're working, really work. If you're loving, really love. Don't waste a minute and you won't waste your life."

How does this philosophy work out in practice? Let's take another look at the runaways mentioned in this book.

* * *

Shadow was born in Harlem, where he lived with his alcoholic father and his prolific mother, who were each too busy fighting poverty and prejudice with both hands to give their children the understanding and affection they needed to help them overcome the same enemies. When his mother was pregnant with her sixth child, Shadow left home to make room for it. Although his parents grieved silently, they were somewhat relieved to have one less mouth to feed.

What would have become of Shadow if he hadn't run away? Chances are his life would not have been much better. He had so many strikes against him from the start. Whether he had stayed home or left as he did, he would have had to overcome many difficulties in order to survive. But, despite these problems, Shadow seems to know how to enjoy himself under the most adverse circumstances.

This appears to be true for many blacks in our society. The stereotype of the black as always happy is, of course, ridiculous, but they do seem to have a more healthy psychological approach to life on the whole, an enthusiasm and a zest for life that so many years of struggle have failed to extinguish.

And, it is difficult to argue the fact that black culturd has had a great influence on all of the young. Youth is drawn to black music, black slang. Young whites try to imitate blacks in many ways.

Another desire shared by many of our youngsters is to live their lives so that they won't be burdened with regrets. It's easier, they feel, to regret something you did than something you really wanted to do but never tried. At least you avoid that monster—what might have been.

The last time I saw Shadow was about a year ago. He spent some time with Randy, Raphael, and me shortly before Randy took off with Judy.

One day Shadow asked Randy if he could borrow a shirt. Randy loaned him his best shirt, a beautiful olive-green one. Shadow wore it that one day. When Randy asked for it back, Shadow told him he had torn it up to make handkerchiefs because he had a bad cold. Randy was broken-hearted over losing his good shirt to such a worthless cause, but Shadow couldn't understand Randy's reaction. "It's just a shirt," he told him.

But it was my favorite shirt," Randy insisted.

You'll get another favorite shirt," Shadow said. "Man, don't waste your head on a lost shirt."

Randy, too, had been unhappy at home, and didn't want to waste his life in a place where he felt he couldn't be happy. He had run away to find himself and to prepare for the revolution, and had found other "parents" who didn't make as many demands on him, demands he felt had violated his integrity. He was still free to go home, look for new parents, become an adult, or disappear. He had tried to become an adult by taking care of Karen and Valerie and other runaways.

Randy's concept of a family is shared by many of our young. They see family not as blood relatives or people held together by legal papers, but as people who care for and care about and thus feel very deeply for each other.

Karen feels she is better off now in the foster home than she was when living with her aunt. Her best friend Valerie is in reform school, making plans for a job-training program. She, too, feels she grew as a result of her runaway experience; that she is much wiser and better prepared to face the vicissitudes of life.

Both Karen and Valerie demanded recognition as adults with adult perogatives. If the laws against runaways were not so repressive, these two might have had an easier time and found the help they needed.

Judy, the girl with whom Randy fell in love, was a runaway from a small town who had left behind a middle-class Italian family. According to Randy and Judy, her father was a member of the Mafia and not above using Mafia tactics on his own daughter. When she ran away, she claimed to be eighteen years old but her father told the runaway squad she was only fourteen.

Judy fell under the battered child syndrome, and you will recall that when she and Randy fell in love, her father threatened to kill them both. The last I heard of Judy, however, she had left Randy to return to her father. Apparently she was involved in a sadistic-masochistic relationship with him that hadn't been worked through yet. She speaks of hating him and actually fearing him, but she respects him and her deep love draws her back to him. The fact that she chose to become involved with someone like Randy, who was relatively timid, rather than a more aggressive person who would not be afraid to stand up to her father seems to prove this. With Randy she did learn a few things about how to survive without parental protection, tested her courage, and developed a better sense of her own identity.

Frances had the strength and toughness to take what she wanted from life. She was able to discard the values of her background and replace them with new ones that seemed to be more adaptable to her needs. She is having a day-by-day love affair with life.

After years of struggling to survive the hard way, Karla finally decided that what she really wanted out of life was what she had run away from—what her parents had. In a way, Karla is going against the tide. The development of the women's movement is rapidly changing our society so that today many men resent having to feel responsible for a woman. The institution of marriage is in trouble, and while most young people are avoiding its bond, Karla is looking for a man to take care of her.

Karla is bound to be unhappy until she realizes that she has to make her own life; that unless she can find her own meaning for life and her own inner fulfillment, marriage cannot possibly provide her with the traditional happy ending. Only when she can see herself as a strong adult will she have a chance at making a marriage that has a chance to survive in these times.

When Karla went back home Netty, her friend in the commune, became a call girl. She fell in love with another black man and began making plans to leave the country with her new boyfriend and her two kids. Netty saw that some planning in the middle-class sense was necessary but she carried it out in an unconventional way. She made her dream come true faster because she had learned to live cheaply and to manipulate opportunity to her advantage during her runaway years.

The birth of Cindy's baby was the push needed by both Cindy and her mother. They straightened out their lives and developed a new respect for each other that might never have happened if Cindy hadn't run away.

Solomon still roams the streets playing his guitar, taking more and more speed and getting farther and farther out in space. His life has been a race with death and therein lies the thrills. Apparently he has a deep guilt about his freedom and is killing himself in order to pay his dues. His family wanted him to produce and he is doing what they asked in the sense that he is constantly writing songs and poetry. He has, however, a pessimistic view of life and sees death as a goal. Of course, Solomon is getting what he wants out of it all—knowledge through suffering and pain. He is our truth-seeker. His trip is enhanced by his notion of death as the great fix. Heaven to him is the ultimate overdose.

Larry Cole, head of the lower East Side Action project on East Sixth Street says, "If you're looking to die, which a lot of street kids accept pretty openly, then you might as well die happy. That's the advertisement for dope. And kids are going to buy that message until we find a way to let them live happy."

Running away was not the right answer for the super-intense Josie, but for Bunny it was an exciting and informative break in her relatively middle-class-future oriented life that sparked her imagination years later and led her to her vocation, anthropology.

The last I saw of Little Bit, she had moved to a commune with a boyfriend who, she felt, was meant for her. Her main trip was sexual and for the time being she had found a relationship that satisfied her. He was older and helped her to grow and expand her ideas and experience new life-styles. She would have been one of the girls who got married to get away from home if she'd been born earlier when marriage was still the way.

Michelle didn't so much run away as she was thrown away, by both her parents and the school system that was unable to teach her reading and writing even though she was of normal intelligence and, in fact, eventually able to teach herself to read and write. She had originally become involved in radical demonstrations on the lower East Side because they were exciting and a natural concomitant of her life-style. Gradually, she began to understand the contradictions within our society, especially the injustice of our involvement in Vietnam and an American prosperity largely based on the exploitation of other nations and a war economy. She had progressed from peaceful demonstrations to guerrilla warfare, and the realization that she had all along been "a mercenary in someone else's war.". After all, through her career as a radical she had had little or no part in decision-making or planning and leading actions because she was a female. Michelle began to see all men as the enemy, a superior class oppressing an inferior class very much on the white/black model and probably preceding it in history. Eventually she realized that this analysis, too, was partial, and that in order to grow she must continue to experience and change.

*   *   *

How can we prevent some of the tragediex awaiting future runaways? What can we as parents and as members of society do?

Our concept of adolescence is a social one that has little relation to the actual needs and emotions of young adults. They long to experience the "real" world, to have meaningful work, to make their own decisions, to have some influence on our laws and customs.

Adolescence is a twentieth-century creation. In early American times one's responsibility for self-support came shortly after physical maturity and sometimes before. John Paul Jones, who received his naval commission at the age of fourteen and was the veteran of several sea battles at sixteen, was no exception to the times.

Today's adolescent endures a time of feeling individual maturity without social recognition of the fact. The young are kept in a prolonged adolescence and held down in sexual and economic competition. School is considered the proper occupation until eighteen and in the case of college students, until twenty-five. Financially and emotionally, the parents' home remains the center for many students; the job market requires a B.A. for well-paid positions. Although our young are educated and shown their potential, they are told they must wait years to put it to practical use.

The ghetto youth often has a different sort of problem. Restless in a decaying school system, he finds himself thwarted in a search for work by the very laws originally intended to stop child-labor exploitation.

Larry Cole of LEAP says, "Compulsory education has become the legal tool by which children are forced into the system...Poor kids' schools do active damage to active minds, but kids are still forced by law and order to attend under the penalty of law."

At an underprivileged school in Harlem, they used to test the intelligence of all the children at two-year intervals. With each test, the children's I.Q. dropped. According to Paul Goodman, author of *Growing up Absurd,* "The combined efforts of home influencing and school education, a powerful combination, succeed in making the children significantly stupider year by year; if they had a few more years of compulsory home ties and compulsory education, all would end up as gibbering idiots."

We spend a great deal of money compelling kids to go to school who do not want to and do not profit by it.

Beginning with school, if not before, children are stripped of their imagination, creativity, heritage, dreams, and personal uniqueness in order to prepare them to fit into a mass, technological society.

Charles A. Reich in *The Greening of America,* calls the labor of school-children labor "an ordeal that both keeps the child off the streets and trains him in the carrying out of prescribed tasks. School is intensely concerned with training students to stop thinking and start obeying.

"The purpose of teaching is to help the student to think for himself. The purpose of indoctrination is to compel him to accept someone else's ideas, someone else's version of the facts."

Eda Le Shan's famous book *The Conspiracy Against Childhood,* says that education overemphasizes I.Q. at the expense of personality, and technical skills at the expense of human relationships.

The students' knowledge of the new and interesting and relevant goes ungraded while their knowledge of the old, distant material is thoroughly examined. They begin to ask why they are studying at all. In their quest for an education that will prepare them for an uncertain, unforeseeable future, the young reject the idea that a school or college is the only possible institution that will supply it.

But parents are upset when their child tries to find himself on his own. What can they tell the neighbors? How do you tell your friends that your son or daughter is farming or fishing in Mexico, or working on an ocean steamer, or waiting on tables in an L.A. coffee shop, or picking fruit with migrant laborers, or meditating in India? Their disapproval shows through. Why isn't he or she in school? Why couldn't they make it in college, or why couldn't they get a good job?

Schools, in most cases, are prisons where artificialities deaden young minds. Our young feel they no longer want to conspire in the hypocrisy.

Our education system needs to be revamped if schools are not to remain a waste of time for our children. They need to learn theory by experiment and doing, to learn belonging by participation and self-rule. We need permissiveness in interpersonal expression, an emphasis on individual differences, an unblocking and training of feelings by means of plastic arts, dramatics, tolerance of races, classes, and cultures. We need to take youth seriously as an age in itself, to recognize the community of youth, make educational use of the actual physical plan and culture of the school community, emphasize the real problems of a wider society and its geography and history, actually participate in the neighboring community.

But, as Paul Goodman says in *Growing up Absurd,* "The problem is not to get them (the young) to belong to society, for they belong a priori by being the next generation."

Mr. Goodman points out that "young people are not taken seriously as existing, as having real aims in the same world as oneself. So, in despair, the fifteen-year-olds hang around and do nothing at all, neither work nor play, without a worthwhile project, without a sense of justification. The made play of the Police Athletic League is not interesting, is not their own. They spend a vast amount of time doing nothing.

When one does nothing, one is threatened by the question, Is one nothing?"

Many youngsters don't know what they want to do when they grow up. Too many answer, "nothing." Well-intentioned public spokesmen don't mention the problems of the young; they are not taken seriously. It is hard to grow up in a society where one's important problems are treated as nonexistent. It is hard to belong to it. It is hard to fight to change it.

Larry Cole of LEAP writes, "There's nothing so crazy-making as someone telling you that your pain isn't real, that what you see before you is really something else."

He feels that this attitude in our society is one important cause of drug addiction in our youth.

Mr. Cole says, "There will have to be a huge effort made at preventing drug use and it isn't going to come out of the present horror story-punishment approach. It's going to come by offering kids more personal and satisfying ways out of their minefields. It will start by adults acknowledging the minefields' existence, waking up from the fogginess of old American dreams, and risking some empathy with the perceptions and condemnations of our youth."

Drugs do exactly what youth wants and exactly what adults don't want; they free the user from some of the pressure for conformity, and they cause the absoluteness of cultural values and ideals to appear even more foolish than they did before.

And the way the society as a whole reacts to youth's experiment with drugs alienates them even further and drives them still deeper into the drug culture. The doubtful effectiveness of the police drug raids, the newly found and often politically motivated zeal for enforcing the drug laws, the apparent focus on minors who use grass, all of these have produced among young people a cynicism about drug laws and their enforcement.

Billy Graham wrote in his book, *The Jesus Generation*, "One of the great drug experts in America told me recently that the only certain cure for drug addiction that he had found was a religious experience."

A child who feels completely alienated may feel a close bond to his peers. Today as never before the young see themselves as part of a generation, a subculture with its own beliefs, life-style, and attire. They see themselves as part of Abbie Hoffman's Woodstock Nation, the Rock Culture, the Age of Protest, Rebels with a Cause, living in McLuhan's Global Village.

The media has glorified youth, has made them models of goodness, glorified their life-style, ways of dress, ways of thinking. It has shown them as flower children, lovers of peace, a family of understanding communalists awaiting with outstretched arms their brothers and sisters who are still "prisoners of home or school."

John Leo, of *The Christian Herald*, points to the counterculture of youth as being born of affluence, mobility, and prolonged adolescence. "A society that keeps its young out of approved adult roles until the age of twenty-one or twenty-two, produces children at a rate that makes them half the population, and then supplies them with enough money to create and respond to its own economic markets, is doing nothing less than spawning a new culture."

More than half our population is under twenty-five.

Earlier, young people such as the beats took the first step to reject the conventional values of American society; today's counterparts are taking the second and are actively searching, sometimes in vain but often with success, for other character values that fit its conception of what humanity should be.

When the beats appeared on the American scene in the fifties, loudly protesting the social values of the time, they were attacked, rridiculed, and subjected to a lot of publicity.

Kerouac's *On the Road* typifies the sense of detachment and perpetual movement associated with the beats. His characters hitch-hiked around the country, made love in a casual way, and generally refused to commit themselves to a sense of community with any group. They have greatly influenced the present generation of youngsters.

Beats, drugs, cool jazz, interracial sex and Zen Buddhism are means of rejecting all things 100 percent American. Our young lean to values such as artistic integrity, voluntary poverty, and social disengagement. They are self-appointed outcasts, perpetual strangers to adult society.

The beatniks led to both the hippies and the New Left. Thousands of kids dropped out of our system. They lived from hand to mouth, off money from home or earnings from panhandling, selling drugs, occasional jobs, and freeloading. They started communes or lived in crash pads, with each person contributing what he or she could.

Entire villages of hippies have sprung up throughout the country. Cities have neighborhoods populated mostly by young runaways and street people. A syndicated newspaper organization connects these separate communities.

Stores and restaurants catering wholly to hippie buyers are found in most urban scenes.

Allen Katzman in *Our Time,* said, "The communes were actually the first manifestations of the change in bohemian trends in America. Until then this was basically a very lonely trip with the exception of the junkies and speed freaks that always stuck together."

People are together when they experience the same thing in the same way. Many of the communes that have sprung up in various parts of the country are based on shared values, such as a love for desert sunsets or drugs, a common religion, the preferred living arrangement, an extended family. Contempt for the technologically centered culture led many to create rural communes where they grow their own food, manufacture their own tools and comforts, and make their own rules.

One of the main reasons for living in a commune is the positive experience in the community, the guarantee that someone will always accompany you on the journey into and through yourself, and when you need someone, someone will be there. Another invaluable function of the commune is sharing your private visions with a companion who cares. These kids share the same heros, like the same movies, read the same books, mostly comics.

Wilhem Reich, the orgone theorist new communalists read most avidly, calls for a sexual revolution. An end to premarital chastity by adolescents and the abolition of concern for marital fidelity are prerequisites for a postrevolutionary sane society, according to the Reichian view.

The expanded family can be simply a close friendship of trust and respect. It may be a convenient symbiotic arrangement involving some mutual baby-sitting and perhaps shared outings or vacations. It can involve friends who rent apartments in the same building, friends who set up a home together, a fully fledged commune, or a group marriage.

The basic doctrine is "do your own thing."

Charles A. Reich says, "The whole emerging pattern, from ideals to campus demonstrations to beads and bell bottoms to the Woodstock Festival, makes sense and is part of a consistent philosophy. Its emotions and spirit can be comprehended only by seeing contemporary America through the eyes of the new generation."

Billy Graham describes these young "who believe in the integrity of the here and now, in work as pleasure, as craftsmanship, in instinct, mystery, joy, accidents, adventure. They wear liberated costumes not for parade but for sheer comfort; do not judge, accept. Share rather than merely compete. They love each other, are not ashamed to weep and to laugh only when they feel like it."

"Technology," as Charles A. Reich points out, "demands a new individual responsibility for values, or it will dictate all values. And it promises a life that is more liberated and more beautiful than any man has known, if man has the courage and the imagination to seize that life." He feels that's what our youth are trying to do.

These young people are responding to a changing world. They speak of the bomb, the Vietnam War and its effects on our culture, the law, racial and religious prejudices, women's rights, and the sexual revolution. Together they form the youth movement, the youth culture, a relatively new phenomenon. Throughout the world young people feel closer together than ever before. Young hitchhikers smile at approaching cars and at each other on the street. They have discovered their need for one another. They make eye contact. When groups of youngsters gather, whether they are hippies, blacks, or draft-resistors, they call each other brother and sister. The young are growing up in a global village and searching for a global identity. What this younger generation has is a way of being with each other that is closer, warmer, more open, more sensitive, more capable of sharing than any previous generations have known.

The young people are reacting to a society that has devalued human

relations, that has subordinated them to an acquisitiveness and competition that has led to affluence and lineliness. Many youngsters are
actually learning to live on a modest scale in order to maintain the
economic freedom they desire. Youngsters seemingly conventional in
every way, are changing their hair styles, clothes, habits, interests, entire
way of life.

They choose clothes that give them more freedom of movement, more
comfort, and if they dress for beauty, it's in bright colors and flowing
skirts. Most of them, however, are not willing to sacrifice comfort for
beauty.

"The costumes of the young," says Charles Reich, "are not masks.
They are expressions of an inner, perhaps momentary state of mind.

"These costumes do not hide the real person as role-dress does, they
show a state of mind and thus reveal him (or her) to us. These new clothes
express profoundly democratic values. They reject competition."

Music has become the deepest means of communication and expression for the entire culture. As outsiders, members of the youth
culture themselves, the bands become groups with which the young
audiences can identify; they share drugs, clothing, attitudes, and values.

Mark Gerzon, author of *The Whole World Is Watching*, says "Today's
psychologically oriented generation criticizes modern society because it
has seen that, in spite of all the emphasis put on individuality and
happiness, society has nevertheless made the individual feel that the
purpose of his life is perseverance in his work, in his striving for social
success, in his endeavor to keep pace with the socially ideal personality.

"If adult society is not aware of the loss of self, it is not surprising that
it finds unreal the search for self. And traveling to communities where
there are other young people working, involving themselves with people,
often taking drugs, sometimes reading books of social criticism, or
psychology or of Oriental philosophy. What was so tragic in most of
these cases was that this process of gaining an identity went unrecognized
and was criticized by these young people's parents."

The search for meaningful character ideals has always been part of
religion. Gerzon points out, "Today's young people direct their spiritual
need not to the supernatural, but to the natural, to themselves, to other
men and to nature. In everything that explodes from youth culture this
generation is spreading its belief that, if one is to find ultimate meaning in
life, it will be in the Natural, in Being itself, in what is most deeply and
profoundly and uniquely human."

Today's young cannot hate other countries or ideologies because of
their awareness that we all live under the threat of the mushroom cloud.
Young people cannot be too patriotic about their own country because

they don't fear other people. They foresee the possibility of mechanical world-wide destruction through modern technology.

The young are attracted to Indian music and Oriental philosophies and religions. Eastern thought has come to play a big part in youth culture because it offers the most coherent and complete alternative to mass-society values. By accepting as their goal the achievement of harmony within themselves and with the world, they are stressing that the ultimate concern of their lives is to be found right here. Their god is within them, within each individual. It is part of human, earthly, mortal life.

Obviously, the most logical thing they can do is turn to the opposite of our culture since they are so dissatisfied with it. Coming from the technological, they want the traditional; coming from the West, they want the East. The needs of the young go unanswered in their own culture. All these attributes are more or less lacking in our society but are basic motifs of Oriental thought.

Eastern religions are concerned with man's unconscious and the nature of his behavior. By unifying oneself and perfecting one's awareness, it is possible to reach the ideal state of harmony of peace with oneself and the world.

It is meaningful religion in a society where religion has lost much of its meaning. What society can speak the dictum of turning the other cheek while dropping bombs on Vietnamese villages? How can adults say they believe one thing and day after day live its opposite without even being aware of the conflict? Religion in America seems so hypocritical that young people are compelled to look to other religions. Timothy Leary, Ginsburg, Allan Watts, Herman Hesse, Gary Snyder, these are the cultural heroes of youth who have led them to the East.

The young are not interested in where or whether a man or woman got a degree, or in what his or her income is, but in whether she or he has a happy life and can feel and love. Youth has the supremacy of the individual as a goal while the adult society sees authority as supreme. "In placing human needs and ecology ahead of law, they propose nothing less than a new social order," is how Charles Reich puts it.

Always before, young people felt themselves more tied to their families, to their schools, and to their immediate situations than they did to their peers. Now an entire culture that includes music, clothes, drugs, and attitude distinguishes youth and makes them a group.

The young see that the most important consideration in our world is other human beings, that everyone faces the irrationality of existence, and that in this common bond one can find a reason for living. They know that relating to others is not a luxury, but the essence of human existence.

They are looking for roles that involve them, a full commitment to their work, and through their work, a full commitment to society. This generation's enthusiastic response to civil rights, anti-war movements, the Peace. Corps, ecology allows the young to commit themselves ideologically and emotionally to their beliefs.

Young women and men today want some inherent value in their work. They are not satisfied with mere monetary reimbursement. They want to simplify human relationships, to make them more satisfying. They say: "We want to be free, open, and honest about everything with everyone. We want to be completely free of guilt and shame so that we could even be naked in the presence of any others and find it beautiful and natural."

They ask for opportunities to do worthwhile work, to earn a little money, and have some self-respect; to have some space to bum around in that is not always someone else's property; to have a voice in their own education, new schools that introduce them to new interests; to have more meaningful sex without fear, guilt, or shame; to have a community and a country to be loyal to and feel proud of; to be given autonomy, a voice in their own destiny, to be free.

They want life to make sense. They want to see the underprivileged and unemployable taken care of in such a way that they maintain their self-respect.

Our young people want to know how to free themselves from society's programming, to understand themselves, their capacities, their special talents, to learn what parts of themselves were limited and destroyed by society, how society discouraged their individuality. Their goal is self-awareness.

Mark Gerzon wrote, "The young awareness is unable to accept that men who cannot find peace within themselves will ever find peace with other men; that men who cannot work on the problems of their own minds will ever work on the problems of the world; and that men who cannot communicate with other men will ever communicate with life."

So the young want international cooperation to replace violence, racial and sexual harmony to replace conflict, economic justice to replace inequity, democracy not totalitarianism, population control not explosion, a natural not a plastic environment; in short, they want human fulfillment, a world of peace and love.

"Young people today," says Gerzon, "are asking that a society which professes freedom and equality make these viables realities. In the underground, in hippie papers, hippie communities, or college areas, you see a person-to-person racial equality that is not evident in adult society."

They criticize adult society by attacking its lethargy in domestic matters. The young seem to agree on one point: They do not want to be like their parents, to have a dull job, a dull house, and live only for their children. Yet, they need to learn to communicate with parents even if only by means of shouts and screams.

If religion is to have meaning in today's society, it must be transformed and the young people are doing just that. They are creating a religion of interpersonal relations, their own religion; they find God, their ultimate concern, through love, not their love through God. Love comes first; the way to find life's meaning is through love.

Billy Graham confesses: "Almost every young person I know is caught up in some sort of revolution. It may be hidden and deeply personal or it may be openly active and highly public. Most young people are searching for purpose, meaning, and fulfillment in their lives."

Speaking of Jesus Freaks, he said, "These young people have solved their problems by their commitment to Jesus Christ and their commitment to each other. The hat is passed with a new invention: If you have something to spare, give. If you need, take."

As John W. Aldridge sees it in *The Country of the Young,* "Their need is, and must always be, to reach their parents, to be able to identify with them or do battle with them, and in so doing, to define themselves."

Our society is characterized by extremely rapid change, which increases the distance between generations. Gerzon acknowledges: "Hesitant rather than challenged, unsure rather than enthusiastic, young men turn away from the mirror of adulthood and toward each other in order to discover who they are."

He feels that today's generation gap has widened to the point where the leaders of adult society are forced to ignore not the fringe but the leaders of youth. Parents are so tied to the past that they see their children's actions not in terms of the actual world situation today, but in terms of the ideologies of their own formative years.

Billy Graham sees the causes of the generation gap as: "the natural rebellion of the human heart, the emptiness evident everywhere, the constant erosion and dehumanization of personality by a machine-oriented age, the lack of purpose and meaning, the tragic failure of our educational system which seems more and more to alienate the young, the overriding social problems that have no foreseeable solutions, the failure of parents to live what they preach; the failure of government to understand that the basic gut-level problems facing the nation are not materialistic and social, but moral and spiritual."

At the same time that adults are saying youth hasn't learned the lessons history has to teach, young people are saying that their parents have failed to learn the more important lessons the events of their own lives have to teach.

America has been described many times as a child-oriented society. Europeans often say that Americans live only for their children. We also try to live through them. Women's liberation has pointed out that many women make the mistake of living vicariously, giving up their own hopes and desires in their concentration on their husbands. The same point can be made about many parents—both men and women—who give up on their own ambitions and fix all their hopes on their children, trying to force them to become what the parents would have liked to be.

Not only is this attitude detrimental to the parents who have it, but it's also bad for their children. Even those who refuse to live their lives to please their parents often carry a burden of guilt about failing them. "My parents did so much for me," they will say. "May father worked two jobs to save for my college education. I can't even force myself to finish high school. I see it as a prison, a complete waste of time. A torture. So how could I possibly go to college? But I feel like hell for disappointing my parents."

Author John Aldrige feels, "The children of affluence and permissiveness have a double problem. They have been emotionally as well as intellectually impoverished because the irritant of necessity is missing from their physical environment. They have been so heavily indulged by their parents, have been the recipients of such massive quantities of every kind of unearned largess that they feel no need to ingratiate themselves with their parents in order to win their attention or approval."

Sometimes these parents put so much pressure on the children, living their lives for them, that the children are forced to take desperate methods. Today more and more of them are running away.

No youngster wants to have it made. She or he wants to make it. Middle-class runaways often feel betrayed. They have glimpsed the real possibilities of life, have tasted liberation and love, have seen the promise of the great American dream—a dreary corporate job, a ranchhouse, or a miserable death in war—and they find it unbearable.

They are disturbed by the contrast between their parents' ideals and the way their parents live. Most of them accept their parents' beliefs, but do not accept their hypocrisy. The discrepancy between what could be and reality is too much for them. By the lives they lead parents often give their children the message. Do not live the way we do.

Charles Reich feels that in order to understand the young, we must understand "the promise of life that is made to young Americans by all of our affluence, technology, liberation and ideals, and the threat to that promise posed by everything from neon ugliness and boring jobs to the Vietnam War and the shadow of nuclear holocaust."

In some cases, children are treated as things, adult toys, to fill the vacancy in their parents' lives. "The child of a home with genuine character develops loyalties, but," as Charles Reich points out, "the child of a plastic home is equally at hime in anything; he might as well be on the road."

' When a child is unhappy at home and hears about how others the same age are living their own lives the way they want to live them, the child is tempted to leave home immediately and join the sisters and brothers on the road. The underground sounds very exciting and romantic. •

They can't imagine the problems that these young people have faced and are facing every day. They've never had to worry about basic necessities such as finding food, shelter, and clothing; being hassled by the police because they're out on the streets late at night when they haven't a place to go.

Looking at the statistics on runaways, it is hard to believe that in 1972, a million teen-agers ran away from home. In New York City alone, the Police Department's Missing Persons' Bureau listed more than 12,500 people under seventeen. According to *The New York News* magazine section, "Triple that number to include the unreported missing kids, and you get a more accurate idea of how many lost and confused children are wandering around."ᵛ Today's youth has been dubbed the Runaway Generation.ᴬ

Running away from home was not invented by teen-agers in the middle sixties. Since the age of exploration, boys have run away to sea. For centuries girls have been eloping with forbidden lovers. Children and adolescents have long left home to join the circus or religious groups. Over a thousand years ago, fifty thousand teen-agers ran away from home in one year to fight for a cause they believed in. Historians call it the children's crusade.

As Billy Graham says, "Today we are much concerned about the casual way in which some of our children vanish from home, taking to the highways in search of independence and a taste of reality. Thousands of young people run away each year and adults, not understanding the phenomenon, take each departure as if it was unprecedented. But running away from home is an ancient dodge."

Still, one would have to say that while these traditional cases of runaways were on the whole isolated phenomena, in the middle sixties adolescents running away from home had become a kind of fad, a movement even, or perhaps a migration. This leads to wonder about the reasons for running away in our contemporary American culture that were not present in the past.

Some people have pointed to the fact that many runaways come from broken homes. It is also true that many runaways come from homes where both parents are present. Still, it seems that in a general, if not a particular, sense there is a correlation between the high rate of divorce and the runaway epidemic. Adult men and women are today claiming their independence of the family unit, whereas fifty years ago most people accepted their marriage, no matter how disappointing. Today more and more adults no longer feel compelled to perpetuate a marriage that does not satisfy them. So children, too, begin to wonder why they should remain in a family situation they find unsatisfactory.

In other areas, too, adults are more likely to make changes in their lives when they feel hemmed in by their situations. More people move now than in the past. One out of three families in America moves every year. People change jobs frequently, throw out old possessions and buy new ones, become involved in new fads and hobbies and drop them. The key word is flux. We still find a need to rationalize abrupt changes in our lives, especially major ones like divorce, or a move to another state, but more and more flux begins to seem the norm, a concomitant of our continuing desire to grow. Adolescents, too, often have a desire to change their situation, to move on; but society's rules and regulations make it much rougher on the adolescent than on the adult. It is extremely difficult for them to get a job or rent an apartment.

Even Billy Graham realizes that, "tens of thousands of youths get bugged with home life and find domestic routines a drag, so they leave home. It is part of the restlessness of our times."

Yes, our young, like the rest of us, are knee-deep in future shock, the age of radical change, instant Zen, automatic marriage and divorce.

So the runaway epidemic is not so surprising when we compare it to some other statistics. One out of every three marriages ends in divorce. More parents leave their children than children leave their parents.

Adults who choose to live together have the option of getting a divorce if their situation becomes intolerable. Children, who have no say in choosing their parents or siblings, have no legal means for "divorcing" their family if they feel it's an unbearable situation.

Many of the reasons children give for running away are similar to those adults give for wanting a divorce—alcoholism, physical or mental cruelty, incompatibility, lack of communication, constant arguments over sex and money, a desire to start a new life, the need for independence, hypocrisy, and different life-styles that seem to clash at all levels.

Adults often tease their kids about dates, pimples, shapes, and habits. What is this but mental cruelty?

Children leave home for many reasons, among them parental neglect, broken homes, poor living conditions, unhealthy background, economic deprivation, mental disturbance, and lack of religious training. Or, a kid may run away because the high school principal calls him into his office and expels him for handing out anti-war leaflets or other social documents. A cop may stop a youth on the street, frisk him or her, find a marijuana cigarette, and haul the child off to jail.

Their parents split up. They love their fathers and hate their mothers and the court places them with their mothers. So they run away.

They run away because running away has been glamorized and romanticized. They see friends running away. Running away seems to offer a shortcut to maturity. Running away is often an escape from personal and family problems. A form of adolescent rebellion, it embodies the spirit of individual freedom.

Children often run away after the death of a parent or close relative, divorce, or move to a new community. Runaways have often suffered from frequent separations, a father who travels a lot, or a parent who projects an attitude of rejection.

"I'm personally convinced that no two parents can rear a child entirely alone," says Dr. Sally Provence of Yale's Child Study Center. "Yet young parents have fewer supports for parenting than ever before; it's either drag the kids along or get a sitter."

Today's mobile, push-button society has all but abolished the extended family. Children tend to learn about the world around them vicariously by television.

David Cooper in *The Death of the Family* says, "The bourgeois nuclear family unit has become, in this century, the ultimately perfected non-meeting, and therefore the ultimate denial of mourning, death, birth, and the experiential realm that precedes birth and conception."

Freud preached that the root causes of emotional disturbances were to be found largely in a disturbed relationship between parents and child in early life.

"Refrigerator parents," parents who tend to be intellectual and emotionally detached with a tendency to think in abstractions, can have a seriously damaging effect on their children. Dr. Bruno Bettelheim, the famed psychoanalyst, feels that many children suffer from unconscious rejection by the mother.

"The parents," he says, "tend to deal with the child in a mechanistic way, out of a sense of obligation rather than genuine affection. This is interpreted by the child as feeling he shouldn't be alive."

In *The Conspiracy of the Young,* Paul Lauter and Florence Howe state: "Estimates are that the suicide rate among students is 50 percent higher than that for Americans generally. In one year 90,000 students threaten suicide, 9000 make an attempt, and 1000 succeed."

But, as *The Greening of America* puts it, "At sixteen or seventeen, no matter how oppressive the corporate state, there is still a moment when life is within their grasp."

Mark Gerzon tells us, "We who make them runaway should ask ourselves, from what kind of society are they trying to escape?"

Paul Goodman knows: "We live increasingly in a system in which little attention is paid to the object, the function, the program, the task, the need; but immense attention to the role, the procedure, prestige and profit."

He asks how is it possible to have more meaning and honor in work? To put wealth to real use? To have a high standard of living the quality of which we are not ashamed? To get social justice for those who have been shamefully left out? To have a use of leisure that is not a dismaying waste of 100 million adults?

He says the young are suffering, not getting enough out of our wealth and civilization. They are not growing up to full capacity, not assimilating much of the culture. We need to make an effort to guarantee belonging. Perhaps there has not been a failure of communication. "Perhaps," Goodman says, "the social message has been clearly communicated to the young men and is unacceptable."

If authority had provided an absolute sense of right and wrong that worked for this generation, there would have been no casting about for idealism, no need for drugs to become an adult or campus demonstrations or looking to the Orient for religion.

Goodman has pointed out that "with all the harmonious belonging and all the tidying up of background conditions, our abundant society is deficient in the most elementary objective opportunities and worthwhile goals that make growing up possible. It lacks work, honest public speech and people aren't taken seriously. It lacks the opportunity for youth to be useful. It corrupts the fine arts. It shackles science. It dampens animal ardor. It discourages religious convictions of justification and vocation and it dims the sense that there is a Creator. It has no honor. No community."

We don't show kids how to be useful and how to make something of themselves. Our children are being deprived of the human community. Family mobility, loss of country and neighborhood tradition, the eating-up of all available space for play have taken the environment away from them.

Lack of focus creates empty lives for many young runaways. The day certainly seems long enough to accomplish the few goals set out; but the hours stretch out and disappear. Days, weeks, months are wasted and the lack of incentive increases.

The street culture is useful to the runaway as an orientation and incubation period. It often marks the first time the youth has had to make her or his own decisions. When the time is extended to months and even years, the street life has become an end in itself. A constant search for free food and care ensues. They plan incessantly for an unrealized future, hanging on to hanging out. A routine of panhandling, drinking, bumming cigarettes, and rapping makes one day indistinguishable from another.

One group, the STP family, specialize in this sort of wastrel existence. They alternate between Boulder, Colorado and New York City at irregular intervals. Most of the members have abused LSD to a great extent, then turned to alcohol to drown their overexpanded awareness.

The men see all women as sexually available to the point of being surprised when strange women object to being grabbed. The few girls in the group are used to rough play. Both the hip and straight community view them as a nuisance.

Whether a runaway returns home of her or his own volition, or is brought home by a parent or the police, it is most important that parents give the situation some careful consideration.

In the case of Frances, the young girl who ran away and became a porno movie star, if her parents had attempted to understand her reasons for leaving and to work out a compromise situation, she might have been willing to stay.

When a child returns home, home life should continue as normally as possible; but at the same time the parents ought to realize that something was desperately wrong, which must be corrected if the child is to remain home. Parents of prodigal children should remember the reception given in the Bible and refrain from verbally attacking the child, or virtually imprisoning her as the parents and guardians of Karen and Valerie did. The parents must stop feeling guilty about their youngster's running away. Guild destroys too many relationships and has never been known to improve any. Once a person feels guilt, he or she immediately looks around for someone else to blame. Parents who feel guilt about their children's behavior make desperate attempts to pass the guilt on to the child.

Many parents are quick to seek professional help for their children who run away. They need to realize that, in most cases, the child is not sick or disturbed, only desperate and unhappy. There is seldom anything wrong with the child or with the parents, but there is usually something lacking in their relationship.

In their book, *Children of Separation and Divorce,* Irving R. Stuart and

Lawrence E. Abt give a list of things parents should do when the child is found:

1. Get rid of feelings of hurt, rejection, and resentment.
2. Try to develop an optimistic outlook of life.
3. Clarify your attitudes towards sex, love, and intimacy.
4. If you're divorced, let your children know they are not the cause. Avoid blaming yourself or spouse. Stress the fact that you both continue to love the children.
5. Inform yourself as well as possible on all aspects of sexual behavior in relationship to love and intimacy, and be aware of prevailing sex mores among young people that may affect your child's relationships with his peers.
6. Take into account the child's current needs and development when you provide guidance and sex education. Answer all questions honestly and truthfully.
7. Try to avoid making exaggerated demands on your children.
8. Stop playing the role of the martyr who feels victimized by the child's demands for care and support.
9. Learn to accept disagreements and conflicts as a natural part of all human relationships, and develop methods of conflict resolution that are fair and acceptable to all family member.
10. Respect your child's need for increasing privacy and self-determination with his or her growth toward adolescence. Refrain from excessive prying into their lives.
11. Do not establish excessively high or unrealistic standards of moral and sexual behavior.

Love is recognizing the freedom of love. Parents and young people must respect each other's needs.

Parents should learn to be non-interfering people, to let their child be, to respect the child's right to say no at times to certain wishes and demands.

Parents should show appreciation if their children do something well.

Let your child know you love and respect her or him.

Establish a guideline for the establishment of a climate of mutual help and respect. Try to be honest, truthful, nonjudgmental, and accepting at all times. Try to provide the guidance your children need to inspire them to seek meaningful relationships. Stress love, intimacy, self-disclosure, and respect for the integrity and individuality of others as the prerequisites for meaningful relationships.

In *Today's Teen-agers,* Evelyn Millis Duvall gives these hints:

1. Get on the young person's side and let him or her know you care without overdoing it.

2. Encourage the teen-ager to participate in activities that interest him or her.

3. Serve nutritious meals and make mealtime pleasant.

4. Broaden teen-agers' experience with food in new and interesting ways.

5. Set a good example, set a good table, and set a youngster free.

Allowance can also be a problem. Help your child to develop a healthy attitude toward money. Teach your children to control themselves on the telephone.

Youth's self-confidence comes from the mutual respect family members have for each other, the confidences they share, the parents' faith in the children, and from family approval of youth's activities. Try to be friends with your children. Have a meaningful two-way communication.

Give your children your confidence. They need to feel you trust them. Give them opportunities to develop faith and confidence in themselves.

Children have-less reason for running away when they can make themselves useful and earn their own money; when their sexuality is taken for granted; when the family carries on its business and the children fall into their own pace; when education is concerned with fostering human powers as they develop in the growing child. Give the child plenty of objective, worthwhile activities to observe, do, learn, or improvise.

Some parents have been able to work out compromises with their children so that the act of running away proved to open a door to a better relationship. One such case involved a young black man. Victor was from a middle-class family. His father was in the clothing business, his mother a private secretary. They owned their own home in Queens.

When Victor started letting his hair grow into a huge Afro, wearing beads and sandals, putting up "Black is Beautiful" posters, smoking marijuana, and dating white women, his parents felt he was going too far in both extremes, trying to be too African and at the same time making too many white friends.

After a great many arguments, Victor ran away to live in the East Village. His father found him and brought him home. Victor was unable to convince his parents that it would be best for all concerned if he could continue to live on the lower East Side in his little rundown apartment while maintaining regular contact with his mother and father. He promised to finish high school, to stop smoking, and not to touch any drugs. His parents reluctantly agreed and so far the solution seems to be working out.

In *Today's Teen-agers* Evelyn Millis Duvall asks "Is your child ready to leave home?

1. Is he or she a fairly autonomous individual, capable of standing on

his or her own feet and making sound decisions without too close dependence on the parents?

2. Are your children mature enough to have outgrown their earlier infantilisms?

3. Have they proven their ability to carry real responsibility for themselves and others? Do they carry tasks through to completion?

4. Do they have some earning ability and willingness to work?

5. Does he or she know what to expect of being on his own or her own?

6. Are their plans realistic?

The laws concerning teen-age runaways are a blatant example of discrimination against youth. Desertion on the part of a mate or a parent is grounds for divorce, but it is not a crime per se. In ancient Rome and Greece, a father had the power of life or death over a child, and things haven't changed too much. Criminal negligence is a crime, but if you leave children with a responsible adult you can't be charged with it. Children are still considered property in many senses.

Contact is a halfway house on New York's lower East Side where the staff dedicates itself to helping runaways, especially those with drug problems. According to literature describing their program:

"Many do not see themselves as troubled and in need of treatment except insofar as some concrete service is required. Others may be aware of some upsetting emergency situation or crisis but are not prepared to accept any goal for themselves which includes commitment to examination of life-style and possible modification or change.

"The treatment program, therefore, takes these various complexities and degrees of readiness into account with a graded and phased program which is also individualized to provide maximum motivation where the client is at the moment."

Kids get into trouble with the law for many reasons. Many petty thefts and burglaries are desperate attempts to feel grown-up. Or, they may be a shortcut to glamour.

Kids play truant and quit school, many as soon as they can. And young people are disturbed by the law's discrimination against race and class. Goodman reminds us, "Upper-class boys almost never get to courts; white boys are dismissed; Negro or Spanish boys are put away." Realities of the "invisible" American sickness.

Today young people share values in some degree hostile to American law. Most of them smoke marijuana, demonstrate, make love, skip classes, beat curfews, drive fast, liberate food or clothes, violate laws or regulations that could send them to juvenile court.

They are subject to harassment if they insist on unconventional behavior, dress, or long hair.

Those who were clubbed by cops in Chicago or Berkeley feel closer to ghetto residents who have been shot or maced or clubbed than to policemen who do such things. They can identify with members of the SLA who were roasted in the L.A. police shoot-in.

Police frish young people and ask for identification if their car is old, the boys' faces unshaven, their hair long, or their dress sloppy. Police and narcotics squads crack down on drug users, which include many, if not most of our young, according to the polls.

Some are arrested for nude swimming or vagrancy. Did you know you can be arrested for nude bathing miles away from any town on a lonely beach?

All the so-called sexual revolution in mass society means is that the division between emotional commitment and sexual involvement has been socially patterned and can now be broadcast through the media and accepted. It is an interrupted revolution. The young know that good sexual satisfaction costs nothing; it needs only health, consideration, and affection. Adults still ponder the question as to whether or not premarital sexuality should be allowed. The real issue in the eyes of the young is not whether sex should be combined with marriage, but whether it is combined with a deep and serious emotional commitment. By emphasizing marriage and sex, parents weaken their argument. If they stressed emotional commitment and sex, the kids would listen.

It should be made easier for young people to lead their own lives. Jobs are not easy for young people to get. The unemployment rate for American youth is higher than for any other industrialized country in the world, has generally run about three times the national average.

Youth are the only ones in the U.S. who can be in violation of the law simply by being where they are. They can be stopped by the police for being out of school; it's called truancy. If they are away from home without permission, it's called running away. When they are out of their houses after a certain hour, it's called violating a curfew. A curfew would be martial law if applied to adults.   An increasing number of youngsters are brought into juvenile court just because their life-style and their set of values are not the same as those of their parents, their school, or the business-and-future-oriented middle-class culture against which they rebel.

Jean Strouse writes in *Up Against the Law,* "Since kids are not considered responsible for criminal behavior, they are called delinquents or juvenile offenders rather than criminals and are to be rehabilitated rather than punished, although a reform school sentence, even if it is called rehabilitation, is still experienced as punishment.

"And since they are not considered criminals, kids have until recently been granted few of the criminal's constitutional rights to fairness and due process of law, the rights, for example, to be represented by a lawyer, to have a jury trial, to refuse to answer questions, to be given written notice of charges, etc."

She points out that some local, state, and district courts are now deciding that students should be seen as people in the eyes of the law; that they do have the right to peaceful protest, freedom of the press, long hair, free speech, due process of the law, and the other rights guaranteed adults.

Many students don't know about their constitutional rights. Or they assume these rights do not apply to kids. Or they don't know that they can take legal action against teachers and school officials who abuse their rights. Since students are not citizens, they have no civil rights. But when the criminal suspect is up against the combined forces of cops, courts, lawyers, and prisons, he has a right to "due process of law," which is often denied the youthful offender.

"Not only do minors have fewer constitutional rights than adults," says Jean Strouse, "because they are considered less than citizens, but they are also liable to be punished for more offenses than adults are, running away from home, disobedience, staying out late, associating with bad companions, being late for school, wearing long hair, publishing opinions critical of a school principal, etc.

"If one watches the juvenile-court process in action, you see that instead of creating the flexibility, individual attention, and leniency that was intended and needed under juvenile laws, the lack of specific standard and protection have produced a legal system that is arbitrary, impersonal, and punitive."

"If a kid is a lonely runaway without domicile or means of support, it takes no great wisdom to infer that he has left a cruel or drunken home or a situation of intolerable uselessness and boredom or that he is ashamed," said Paul Goodman in *Growing up Absurd*. "Provide him with something worthwhile and give him solace."

Our society has arbitrarily decided that its children come of age on the magical eighteenth birthday. From this day forward, they are presumably free to lead autonomous lives. Before that the parents are responsible for them, and they are responsible to the parents. In reality, of course, each person matures at a highly individual pace. It is obviously absurd to say that one becomes an adult on a specific day.

But our culture has made a fetish of the passing of years, which is why many people find it disconcerting to see a stolid self-contained ten-year-old (cute, precocious) or a rebel over thirty (sick, disgusting). Such people mock expectations that are reinforced by the media. These myths pertaining to the expected roles for people of different ages help to orient people. So do myths pertaining to expected roles for people of different races or sexes; like the racial and sexual role myths, those pertaining to age must be discarded.

The accepted idea that young people under eighteen must be constantly supervised and incessantly advised for their own good does not have any proven validity unless you are talking about toddlers. It has simply been assumed to be necessary, to the detriment of adolescents and ultimately to the society, since they in time become the society.

The assumption is upheld by law, not mere custom. If you are under eighteen and decide that life with your parents is intolerable, you can forcibly be returned to them, although the same cannot be done to a parent who abandons his or her children. If you run away repeatedly, you can be consigned to reform school.

Since running away is rapidly becoming so widely accepted by today's youth, it is vital that we change the statutes that make it a crime. These laws force runaway youngsters into living outside the law. They threaten their physical safety and sometimes their very lives by making them pawns in the hands of pimps, drug dealers, sexual perverts, and others who blackmail them into doing their will with threats of reporting them to the police or offers of food, shelter, or money—necessities that most runaways are unable to provide for themselves legally since they have already broken one law.

Practically all those who deal with runaways—halfway houses, social workers, runaway squads, and judges—agree that the situation as it exists today does not work in the best interests of the runaway, parents, or the people trying to help them. When a law causes more harm than good, it's time to change or abolish it. The laws that make running away from home illegal and harboring a runaway a crime must be changed before more lives are ruined. When the prohibition laws could no longer be enforced, they were reviewed, and they did not directly create and destroy innocent victims the way anti-runaway laws do.

Of course, nobody wants to encourage youngsters to run away. But the cure is not keeping it illegal; it's creating a happy home where a child feels loved and wanted, respected, and free so that he or she develops no desperate need to flee.

Sometimes, just as marriages must be dissolved on the grounds of incompatibility, a child must leave her or his home for this reason. But even then it should be worked out so that the child can go to a safe sanctuary where her or his needs are cared for and the parents don't have to worry that their child has died or been destroyed.

What I have tried to do in this book is acquaint you with a few youngsters who have suffered because of our laws and the general discrimination against youth, in the hope that something will be done to change them before other Karens, Randys, Judys, and Josies succumb to drugs, prostitution, mental illness, or end up in city morgues.

The slayings of twenty-seven boys in Houston has re-emphasized the need for quick Congressional action on legislation to create a system of national runaway houses, according to Senator Walter Mondale of Minnesota and Representative William J. Keating of Ohio. The Senate has passed a bill to establish a nationwide police-reporting procedure to enable parents of runaways to locate their children and to provide halfway houses for runaways. The House of Representatives has yet to act on the measure. Keating urges that the House hearings be held on the bill as soon as possible. The Houston mass killings demonstrate that the problems of runaways or young people believed to be runaways demand constructive action.

According to Mondale, who steered the bill through the Senate, "These murders highlight the potential tragedy facing these troubled children who are estranged from their families."

The bill and its provision of halfway houses would only be one step in the right direction. The police-reporting methods might create more problems than they solve, unless they are accompanied by a repeal of the runaway laws so that the runaways can be helped by the police but not arrested by them.

Even changing all the runaway laws is a stopgap measure until we can create loving homes our children will want to stay in until they're prepared to build their own. But it is an immediate need, and when a house is on fire, you don't discuss how to build a better one until you've done what you can to save the one you have.

Children are our most precious possessions. Let's save the ones we still have. It's a cold, dangerous, often heartless world out there for eager, trusting, vulnerable kids.